NERD
365

NERD 365

A Year of ~~Op~~**APP-**portunities

to Upgrade Your Life

BETH ZIESENIS
YOUR NERDY BEST FRIEND

Nerd365

A Year of APP-ortunities to Upgrade Your Life

Copyright @2022 Beth Ziesenis

ISBN: 978-1-7341834-2-9

Printed in the United States of America

Your Nerdy Best Friend Ink
Avenue Z, Inc.
11205 Lebanon Road #212
Mt. Juliet, TN 37122
yournerdybestfriend.com

Sarah Katherine Ziesenis is a science teacher.

She is a mom,

a wife,

a daughter,

a reader,

a crafter,

a gardener

and an introvert.

She's also the best sister anyone could ever have.

For Sarah:

My Very Best Friend

Shout Outs

• •

These days we have AI writing assistants (Page 54) that can create great copy with just a few prompts and keywords from us, but it's not quite advanced enough for this type of book. I did all the research and wrote every word myself. But because of my friends, family and staff, I never felt alone.

Thanks to everyone who helped me along the way, with a special shout out to these extraordinary human (and nearly human) beings:

- They who believed in this book before it was finished and ordered in advance:
  My NerdHerd (I love these folks! See their names starting Page 239)

- He who put up with my histrionics as I stressed out over the book:
  Husband D.J. Rausa

- She who kept my business going while I focused on the book:
  Manager Haley Kruse

- She who figured out where all the little cartoons would go as she
  has with all of my books:
  Designer Marian Hartsough

- She who wiggled her tiny, warm, furry body onto my lap as I wrote
  late into the night:
  Roadie Von Peepers, my Quarantine Kitten

Table of Contents

Introduction

Do you get a little hungry when you hear that December 30 is National Bacon Day (not to be confused with International Bacon Day, the Saturday before Labor Day #becausebacon)? Or do you stop to contemplate the environment on Earth Day (April 23)? Or maybe you reach out to a struggling friend during National Suicide Prevention Month (September).

Fun, interesting and downright weird holidays provide opportunities for great conversations and heightened awareness. My love of the recognitions was the idea behind this book.

My goal is to match fun and interesting holidays with apps, tech tools and tips that will help you celebrate.

Unlike my last few books, this is not a textbook of technology tools with detailed overviews and in-depth comparisons. Instead I'm offering share-worthy holidays paired with tested technology and tools you can use right away.

Writing This Book Surprised Me

This is my seventh book about apps and tech tools. When I started, I figured that I'd base the new one on the last book, a strategy I've used for the other books. I assumed I'd be covering the same topics and updating the best tools and rewrite and reconfigure them into the new format.

That's totally not what happened!

As I dove into the thousands of holidays, I used them to inspire the discovery of tech tools I never thought to share or even heard of. For example, I'd never heard of National Use Your Gift Card Day (third Saturday of January). I went in search of a tool that might go with it and found a nonprofit called the Gift Card Bank where you can donate unused cards (Page 177). And Update Your References Week (First Week of May) gave me the opportunity to tell y'all about videoask, a tool that lets you greet website visitors with a video from you and encourages them to send a video testimonial back (Page 81).

This means that this book has resources I've never shared before along with a brand new flow and format.

Introducing Find Your Inner Nerd Day

We were so inspired by all these holidays that we founded one of our own. Mark your calendars for August 23... Find Your Inner Nerd Day!

The author of bestselling books including "The Fault in Our Stars" shared the best description of nerds ever in one of his YouTube videos.

> *"Nerds like us are allowed to be unironically enthusiastic about stuff. Nerds are allowed to LOVE stuff, like, jump-up-and-down-in-your-chair-can't-control-yourself LOVE it.*
>
> *When people call people nerds, mostly what they're saying is, 'You like stuff,' which is not a good insult at all, like, 'You are too enthusiastic about the miracle of human consciousness."*

—John Green
Author, Vlogger, Fellow Nerd

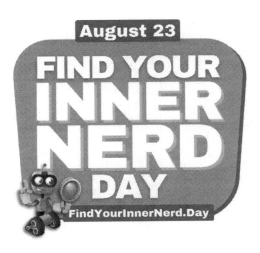

We founded Find Your Inner Nerd Day to inspire you to share what you LOVE — your dog clothes knitting addiction, your Star Wars action figure collection, your bookmarked videos of the Riff-offs from the "Pitch Perfect" movies. We chose August 23 as the recurring date because that's the day Chris Messina posted this simple Tweet in 2007…

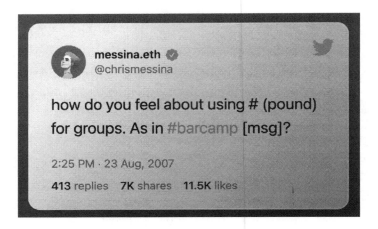

how do you feel about using # (pound) for groups. As in #barcamp [msg]?

2:25 PM · 23 Aug, 2007

413 replies   **7K** shares   **11.5K** likes

And POOF… the hashtag was born, allowing nerds to tag their hobbies and passions so they could find each other and realize they (we!) are not alone.

This QR code takes you to the official page for Find Your Inner Nerd Day, where you can tell us about your nerdy sides and share the holiday.

P.S.: The famous Chris Messina himself gave me permission to use his famous Tweet in this, which he transformed into an NFT and auctioned off for $10k. And true to his generous nerd roots, Chris then donated a chunk of the proceeds to benefit Girls Who Code. #NerdsRock

P.P.S.: Chris also pointed me to **Poet.so**, a site that transforms plain ole' Tweets and LinkedIn posts into shareable graphics.

Poet.so
Site to Make Graphics Out of Tweets and LinkedIn Posts

poet.so

Check Out the Online Calendar

This book is not a calendar that you follow day to day, but since everything is connected to notable dates, we decided you need a calendar to go with it — especially since our own holiday is on it.

This QR code leads you to the real-time calendar on our website. You can check out the fun holidays and the apps to go with them, and you can even subscribe to the calendar feed to add nerdy inspiration to your own schedule.

For every section, you'll see a QR code that will lead you to a page with the dates and tools mentioned in that section.

Resources for Notable Holidays

One of the joys of writing this book was discovering the fun and interesting holidays.

Different notable holidays sites have different treasures, so I checked multiple sources to find the best ones. These five sites are great places to start. In the description I added the celebrations each listed for July 2.

Tip: Google for other sources or original sites for the holidays you choose. Sometimes people make stuff up, you know.

ANGIE GENSLER
JULY 2 HOLIDAYS

Alice Springs
Show Day

I Forgot Day

Made in the USA Day

National Anisette Day

World UFO Day

Angie Gensler

Social Media Content Site with an Insane List of Holidays

angiegensler.com

My friend and fellow speaker Mimi Brown introduced me to **Angie Gensler**. She's a social media guru who helps people create content. And for $96 a year she gives you an insane number of resources and ready-to-post social media content. The tipping point for me to subscribe was a well-researched list of more than 3,200 holidays from everywhere! I discovered all kinds of interesting dates that hadn't shown up elsewhere. Plus her calendar comes with ready-to-post images and an app to keep posting great content on the go. This is seriously worth the price.

Brownielocks

Holiday Site with Tons of Personality

brownielocks.com

Brownielocks is my sentimental favorite site for holidays. It's quirky, whimsical and always up to date. The other sites on this list may have more background and be more user friendly, but I find her use of Comic Sans font (the most hated font in the world) endearing. Don't judge me.

List of National Days

Well Organized Site for Interesting Holidays

listofnationaldays.com

List of National Days calls itself "The 'Official List' of U.S. National Days." I'm not sure who certified this as official, but it is well organized. I like the quick links to popular topics such as Cat Days, Hug Days and Candy Days.

National Day Calendar

Official-Ist Looking Holiday Site

nationaldaycalendar.com

National Day Calendar tracks almost 1,500 national days, weeks and months. They do a great job showing the background of the holidays (great fodder for blog posts) and make it easy to share on social media. Plus they have 3-minute daily podcasts with the daily holidays. Oh yeah, and their food holidays are listed along with recipes to celebrate.

**BROWNIELOCKS
JULY 2 HOLIDAYS**

I Forgot Day

Made in the USA Day

Second Half of the Year Day

World UFO Day

**LIST OF
NATIONAL DAYS
JULY 2 HOLIDAYS**

Build A Scarecrow Day

Foam Blaster Day

I Forgot Day

National Anisette Day

World UFO Day

**NATIONAL DAY
CALENDAR
JULY 2 HOLIDAYS**

International Day of Cooperatives

National Anisette Day

World UFO Day

INTRODUCTION

NATIONAL TODAY
JULY 2 HOLIDAYS

Hop-a-Park Day

I Forgot Day

International Day of Cooperatives

Made in the USA Day

National Anisette Day

National Wrong Trousers Day

World UFO Day

National Today

Holiday Listing Site with Handy Categories and Tags

nationaltoday.com

National Today is a delightful site. Not only does it have a very complete list of holidays, you can see categories such as Crazy, Historical, Drinking, Food and much more.

Like National Day Calendar, National Today offers plenty of background information about the holidays. And they add related holidays at the end (such as National No Pants Day as a suggestion for National Wrong Trousers Day).

Stay Organized

Task Management

Pick Just One Task

Plan

Time-Blocking Task Manager

getplan.co

FEBRUARY 22

Single Tasking Day

In our multitasking world, Single Tasking Day (February 22) asks us to stop trying to do everything and instead get one dang thing done and off the list. Try the **Plan** tool for an easy time-blocking task manager that revamps your calendar so you can actually get things done.

Start a Bullet Journal

**The Bullet Journal®
Companion**

Digital Companion App to the Official Bullet Journal System

bulletjournal.com

OCTOBER 30

**National
Checklist Day**

October 30 is National Checklist Day. The origins of the checklist are a bit grim. In 1935, a pilot overlooked a small task, which resulted in a deadly crash. The result was the standardization of the tasks that must be done every time: A checklist.

Most of us don't make life-saving checklists. We're simply trying to get our you-know-what together. Bullet Journals use checklists and, no surprise, bullet points to organize today, this week, this month and this year. And, of course, there's an app for that.

Like Rocketbook (Page 17) the **Bullet Journal Companion** combines real notebooks and virtual ones. You use it in conjunction with the BuJo® notebook (that's cool speak for Bullet Journal, of course).

Organize Your To-Dos to Stay on Track

The best way to celebrate Get Out of the Dog House Day (the third Monday in July) is to not get into the dog house in the first place. Keep your task list organized with everyone's favorite to-do list: **Todoist**.

Like many of the top task list tools, Todoist lets you sync your lists on any device. Todoist gets extra points for its natural-language task skills (such as "remind me to make my car payment on the first of every month starting in October"), as well as its integrations with automation tools like IFTTT and Zapier.

Alternatives: people adore **Any.do** for its simplicity. I'm fond of the day planner feature that helps you prioritize the day's events. You can also use the gamification incentives with Any.do to make task management fun (kidding—to-do lists are not fun). **TickTick** also gets high marks, but I get anxious about hearing seconds tick away when I read the name.

Any.do

Simple Task Manager with Day-by-Day Manager

any.do

TickTick

To-Do List with Habit-Tracking Functionality

ticktick.com

Todoist

Award-Winning Task Management Tool with a Super Free Version

todoist.com

 JULY

Get Out of the Dog House Day

Third Monday in July

Tracking and Inventory

Put Your Affairs in Order

Cake

DIY Asset Organization with a Free Level

joincake.com

Everplans

Site to Organize Your Finances and Assets

everplans.com

 OCTOBER

National Estate Planning Awareness Week

Third Week in October

The third full week in October is National Estate Planning Awareness Week to encourage people to think about what happens to their assets when they die.

When Mom died, she had emails in her inbox that went unanswered because we didn't have any passwords. No one likes to talk about passwords before we pass away, but these tools can help make things easier for your loved ones to manage your digital life.

> *Note: As I was investigating this section, I stumbled upon a blog post about afterlife sites from 2010. Every single one of their recommended tools was kaput. I don't know about you, but this makes me nervous. What if we put our last requests and final documents into an afterlife app that kicks the bucket before we do? I might just get a big binder and go old school. But anyway....*

You'll be doing your family members a favor if you take the time to assemble the information that **Everplans** recommends. The site will help you create a personalized list of tasks and resources that you own in all kinds of corners of the internet and beyond, such as financial information, medical records, online accounts and legal documents. Everplans also lets you write letters to loved ones that will be sent after, well, you know.

Everplans is $75 a year, but **Cake** has a robust free version. The site steps you through all the documents and decisions you need to make to keep things in order. The name is a little weird, but it has great reviews.

Put Your Affairs in Order (continued)

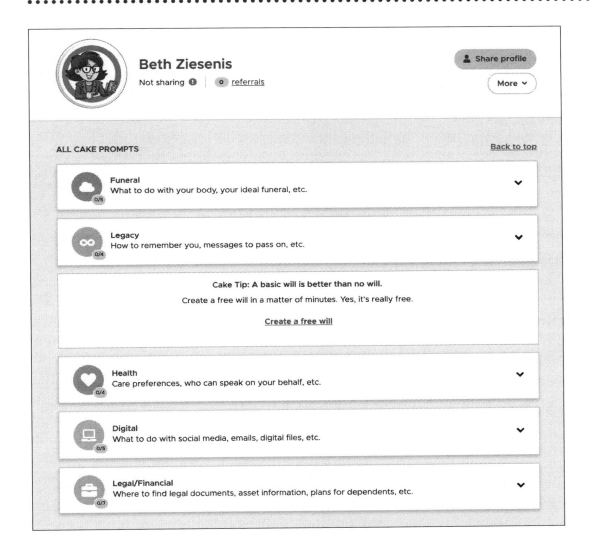

Beth Ziesenis
Not sharing ⓘ | 0 referrals

👤 Share profile

More ⌄

ALL CAKE PROMPTS   Back to top

☁ 0/5
Funeral
What to do with your body, your ideal funeral, etc.   ⌄

∞ 0/4
Legacy
How to remember you, messages to pass on, etc.   ⌄

Cake Tip: A basic will is better than no will.

Create a free will in a matter of minutes. Yes, it's really free.

Create a free will

♥ 0/4
Health
Care preferences, who can speak on your behalf, etc.   ⌄

💻 0/5
Digital
What to do with social media, emails, digital files, etc.   ⌄

💼 0/7
Legal/Financial
Where to find legal documents, asset information, plans for dependents, etc.   ⌄

Track Your Packages

Slice

Package-Tracking Tool with Shopping Help

slice.com

JANUARY

National Bubble Wrap Appreciation Day

Last Monday in January

Everyone knows the joy of popping the cells of bubble wrap, so it's no surprise there's a National Bubble Wrap Appreciation Day (last Monday in January).

Make sure your precious, bubble-wrapped gifts get to you and your recipients with **Slice**, a package-tracking tool.

Declutter Your Office

Sortly

Packing Organization Tool

sortly.com/moving-app

JANUARY

National Clean Off Your Desk Day

Second Monday in January

National Clean Off Your Desk Day is the second Monday in January. Pack up the stuff you don't need and organize it with the **Sortly** app.

Although they are focused on inventory management for businesses, they have a free version that is great for keeping track of home inventory and for moving.

Snap pictures of your belongings as you put them in the boxes, then organize them in the app. Use the app to generate color-coded labels with QR codes for each box. It's easy to find the right box when you need to retrieve an item.

Note Taking and Sticky Notes

Organize Your Sticky Notes

A teenage Canadian girl founded Positive Post-It Day to encourage positive messages for kids in schools to fight bullying. Although the date is a little fuzzy (October 9 or maybe Valentine's Day or maybe February 22 or...), Positive Post-It Day is a good reminder for all of us to rescue the un-sticky sticky notes we have around our monitors and the triple-creased squares sticking out of files.

When you're ready to bring your Post-It collection digital, 3M has an app for that. The **Post-It App** is designed to capture your 3 x 3" brilliance on paper stickies, plus you can create digital ones, share them with your team, access them across devices and generally keep your life together with stickies. Need a step up? Try **Stormboard** for stickies in a mind map environment.

Post-It App

Official Sticky Note Capture and Organizer Tool

nerdybff.com/postitapp

Stormboard

Teamwork-Type Mind Maps with a Sticky Note Look

stormboard.com

OCTOBER 9

Positive Post-It Day

Organize Your Random Notes and Research

Apple Notes
Apple's Note-Taking System
On Apple Devices

Evernote
Everlasting Note-Taking Tool with Limited Free Features
evernote.com

Google Keep
Google's Note-Taking Tool
google.com/keep

Joplin
Open-Source Note-Taking Tool
joplinapp.org

OneNote
Microsoft's Note-Taking Tool
onenote.com

Simplenote
Super Simple Note-Taking Tool from the Makers of WordPress
simplenote.com

APRIL 5

National Flash Drive Day

[The author snores gently then awakes with a start]

Oh, I'm sorry! I was writing about the top note-taking tools, and I nodded off from boredom because the list hasn't really changed in years and years.

Organizing your notes, research, random lists and important images into a cloud-based service is not exactly the best way to celebrate National Flash Drive Day on April 5. But it's an excellent step toward keeping your essential information at your fingertips.

Microsoft OneNote, **Google Keep**, **Apple Notes**, **Evernote**… zzzzzz. They're all excellent options with (very) proven track records. You can't go wrong with any of them, although you'll have to pay for the premium version of Evernote to get the best out of it.

We do have more options these days beyond the classics. The "same page" tools on Page 63 are great options for organizing private and public notes and saved snippets. Project management tools (Pages 64–65) are also excellent for personal use. But if you're looking for something different, try **Joplin** or **Simplenote**. They're both clean, intuitive, beloved and free. We like free.

Capture Handwritten Notes from a Real Notebook

If you're someone who loves the feel of a pen and paper, you'll be happy to hear that National Handwriting Day is January 23.

Rocketbook blends old school handwritten notes with modern technology. You take notes in the smart notebook just like you would in a steno pad. Then you can program the system so you can snap pictures of your notes and immediately send them to wherever you want: Evernote, Dropbox, email and many other options. Once you fill your notebook, you can erase the ink and use it again without losing any notes. What's more, handwriting recognition means your notes are transcribed into editable text.

Rocketbook

Smart Notebook to Save Handwritten Notes to the Cloud

getrocketbook.com

 JANUARY 23

National Handwriting Day

Save Favorite Articles to Read at Your Convenience

May 29 is a great time to celebrate an under celebrated workhorse in the office… National Paperclip Day. If you use the **Pocket** tool, you might not even need to have them in a dish on your desk. Pocket is the most popular "Read It Later" service for saving websites, online articles and more. You can throw resources into Pocket in browsers, on your phone and via a number of connections to other apps. You can even email Pocket things you want to save. The basic version is fantastically feature-rich, and Premium adds smart tagging and full-text searches.

Pocket

Tool to Save Stuff to Read Later

getpocket.com

 MAY 29

National Paperclip Day

Map Out a New Plan

Creately

Online Mind Map Tool with Easy Templates

creately.com

MeisterTask

Task Management Tool with Mind Map Integration

meistertask.com

MindMeister

Mind Map Tool with Task Integration

mindmeister.com

Mindmup

Super Simple, Super Free Mind Map Site

mindmup.com

 APRIL 6

National Sorry Charlie Day

If you're a nerd of a certain age, you might remember StarKist Tuna's official spokes-fish. Charlie the Tuna was always trying to be good enough to be a StarKist tuna, but the announcer would always say, "Sorry, Charlie," which roughly translates these days to "Tough luck, bro."

Charlie was so famous back in the day that he has his own holiday: National Sorry Charlie Day on April 6. Celebrate this day by moving on after something doesn't go your way. To look forward, try a mind map app.

I'm a linear thinker. Give me a traditional outline, and I'm good to go. But lots of you like to balloon one idea after another and connect them in creative ways. Try **Creately** for easy-to-use templates or the **MeisterTask/MindMeister** combo for task management and mind mapping.

And talk about easy… **Mindmup** is your instant gratification mind map site with no registration required.

Stay Focused

19

Distraction Management

Take Back Your Time

Marinara Timer

Online Pomodoro Timer
for Groups

marinaratimer.com

Pomodoro Technique®

Kitchen Timer
Productivity Technique

**cirillocompany.de/pages/
pomodoro-technique**

 FEBRUARY

**National Time
Management Month**

Since February is National Time Management Month, it's time to dive into **The Pomodoro Technique®**.

Hands down the Pomodoro Technique is the very best tool in my focus toolbox. The technique was created by an Italian guy named Francesco Cirillo with a tomato-shaped kitchen timer ("pomodoro" is Italian for "tomato"). He'd set the timer for 25 minutes and focus on ONE TASK... just ONE... for the entire 25 minutes. He'd block out calls, emails, dings, dongs and doorbells. When the timer went off, he'd take a 5-minute break to catch up on other things, then dive back into another 25-minute stretch.

The cool thing about the Pomodoro Technique is that you can do it with a kitchen timer, a fancy app or just the stopwatch on your phone. I have a couple of timers on my Mac. You don't have to complicate things... just set a timer and go. If you want to sync up with colleagues and have a "Pomodoro Party" (I made that up), try the **Marinara Timer** so everyone is focusing on the same schedule.

Dive into Deep Work

October 20 is the National Day on Writing. If you're like me, I need blocks of time to produce words on paper. To write a blog post, book chapter or even an in-depth email response, I need more than a 15-minute break between meetings.

Although **Caveday** is a paid service that starts at about $36 a month, you'll quickly see an ROI by your increased productivity. Caveday is a community that meets for facilitated work sessions for focus and accountability. You sign up for their sessions and let the facilitators guide you through quiet work sprints followed by short check-ins and energy breaks.

Caveday
Guided Focus Sessions via Zoom
caveday.org

 OCTOBER 20

National Day on Writing

Block Out Your Distractions

Don't wait until the last workday of the year to invoke the spirit of No Interruptions Day. Use distraction management tools all year long to limit your time-sucking websites and avoid checking your phone every 10 minutes. **Stayfocusd** and **BlockSite** are browser plugins that help you limit time you spend on shopping sites, social media and other internet black holes. Bonus… both have a sassy sense of humor to make you smile when you get caught getting off track.

BlockSite
Free (and Funny) Distraction Helper for Devices and Browsers
blocksite.co

Stayfocusd
Simple Website Blocker with an Attitude
stayfocusd.com

 DECEMBER

No Interruptions Day

Last Workday of the Year

Put Your Phone Away

Forest

App to Help You Break Your
Phone Addiction

forestapp.cc

Little Free Library

Network of Mini Libraries
Constructed by Volunteers

littlefreelibrary.org

National Day of Unplugging

Site with Ideas for
Screen-Free Activities

nationaldayofunplugging.com

 MARCH

**National Day of
Unplugging**

First Friday of March

The first Friday of March is an observance this nerd finds almost impossible to celebrate: **National Day of Unplugging**.

You can take the pledge to unplug your devices for 24 hours and even get your own smartphone "napsack." Another cool activity the organizers promote is a scavenger hunt in August with your local **Little Free Libraries**.

You can also make a pact with the **Forest** app that you'll leave your phone untouched for a certain period of time. Succeed and Forest rewards you by growing digital trees. Fail and you kill a tree. The choice is yours.

Time Tracking

Be Honest About Where Your Time Goes

April 30 is National Honesty Day, and maybe it's time to be honest about your productivity. If you're constantly wondering "Where did today go?" you might be ready for **RescueTime**.

This software runs on your computer and keeps track of every second you spend on your device and every place you spend it. You'll see time reports for how long it took you to finish a document in Microsoft Word and how many minutes you spent surfing cool cupcake pictures on Pinterest. Sadly, they took the free version off the table, but it falls under #worththeprice.

If you're not good at keeping track of time yourself, give **Toggl** a try. Just click the timer once when you start a project and again when you finish. Toggl keeps track of your work hours to help with hourly billing and time management. And if it senses you're working without tracking or you stopped and forgot to turn off the timer, Toggl gently reminds you.

RescueTime
Software that Tracks Where the Time Goes
rescuetime.com

Toggl
Time-Tracking Tool for Clients and Projects
toggl.com

 APRIL 30

National Honesty Day

Countdown to Important Dates

Time and Date

Site for Countdowns, Time Zone Help and Calendars

timeanddate.com

 MARCH 21

National Countdown Day

Create your own countdown with a beautiful background on the cool site called **Time and Date**. This is a great way to celebrate National Countdown Day every March 21.

Time and Date has all kinds of cool features beyond the custom countdowns. You can find the best time to schedule an international meeting and calculate the number of business days left in the year (excluding holidays and weekends automatically). You can also create custom calculators and even peruse fun and wacky holidays.

How many days until **Find Your Inner Nerd Day** (Page 3)? Check it out with this QR code.

Automation

Automate the Little Tasks

Let's talk about tools that automate tasks so you don't have to work as hard. I didn't know whether to associate tools like **IFTTT** and **Zapier** with National Lazy Day (August 10) or Work Like a Dog Day (August 5).

When you automate your tasks, you can stop working like a dog and get a little lazier because work is done for you.

Without even realizing it, you probably do the same tasks over and over, such as checking the weather, saving attachments from emails, tweeting your latest blog post on Twitter.

Though it takes just a few minutes to complete each task, these little jobs add up fast, and you probably have better uses of your time in today's crazy-busy lifestyle.

Zapier and IFTTT, which stands for "if this then that," are two of the tools that will help you automate some of these little tasks so you don't have to think about them. Just connect your cloud-based services, social media accounts, phones and more, and create little recipes ("Zaps" with Zapier and "Applets" in IFTTT) that trigger under your rules.

They both work with several devices and gadgets, venturing into the world we know as "The Internet of Things." You can automate tasks with smart thermostats, Philips Hue light bulbs and many fitness trackers. You can also create opportunities to use specific iOS and Android features, such as location tracking and selfies.

My favorite party trick: Set up an IFTTT applet to ring your phone with a touch of a button to get you out of a boring meeting.

IFTTT

O.G. Multi-App Automator

ifttt.com

Zapier

Extensive Multi-App Automator with Paid Levels

zapier.com

 AUGUST 5

Work Like a Dog Day

 AUGUST 10

National Lazy Day

STAY FOCUSED

Create Automations on Your Mobile Devices

Shortcuts
Apple Device Automator
In the App Store

Tasker
Android Device Automator
In the Google Play Store

JULY 14

Pandemonium Day

On July 14, I urge you to use technology so that you don't have to participate in Pandemonium Day! Tools like IFTTT and Zapier (Page 25) set up workflows for work and home, but you also have that ability in the palm of your hand.

Tasker and **Shortcuts** are automators that make your mobile devices more efficient. You can set up little automations to run for common phone tasks, such as reading the news (have Siri read it to you), posting to Facebook, combining photos into a GIF, letting meeting attendees know you're running late, and much, much more.

Tasker fans have become a little cranky in the reviews lately, with a common complaint about how complicated it can be to set up a task. Shortcuts has glowing praise and lots of pre-set templates.

Let Artificial Intelligence Plan Your Schedule

Motion
AI-Powered Organizer for
Calendars, Meetings and Tasks
usemotion.com

Trevor AI
AI-Powered Scheduling
Assistant that Organizes Tasks
and Appointments for
Maximum Efficiency
trevorai.com

JULY 2

I Forgot Day

In the high-tech world we inhabit, I Forgot Day (July 2) is no longer a good excuse for missing a meeting.

Tools like **Trevor AI** and **Motion** use artificial intelligence to manage and plan our schedules so our appointments are optimized, organized and impossible to forget.

Outsourcing

Find an Extra Set of Hands

Admins around the globe keep the world spinning, and Administrative Professionals Day is the day to sing their praises (ok, you should be thanking them all day, every day, but especially at the end of April).

We could all use a little more support, and you have out-sourcing options galore in today's tech-connected world.

My favorite support team, **Fancy Hands**, employs a stable of U.S.-based virtual assistants who take annoying little tasks off your list so you can concentrate on getting work done. Fancy Hands helps me set appointments, track down lost mail, transcribe business cards, create cool graphics, research tech tools—you name it—all kinds of little 20-minute tasks that can take me out of work mode and make me lose more time. Prices start at $18 a month for up to three tasks.

Need to build a new website? Or create a fancy intro video that makes your logo dance? Or revamp your marketing material? **Fiverr** is a marketplace of thousands of people who do all kinds of stuff—starting at five bucks (a fiver, get it?). These days you'll find lots of pros that charge much more than $5, but it's because they're truly professionals.

For bigger projects, check out **Upwork**. Describe your project and set the parameters: your budget, your time-line, your hopes and dreams for a successful project. Then you open your project for bids to the marketplace. To find the right person, you might want to search the providers and invite your favorites to bid. If you're commissioning an illustration, for example, hop around in their portfolios to find a designer with a style you like.

Fancy Hands

U.S.-Based Virtual Assistants for Small Tasks

fancyhands.com

Fiverr

Freelance Marketplace for Small Jobs Starting at Five Bucks

fiverr.com

Upwork

Freelance Community for Larger Projects

upwork.com

 APRIL

Administrative Professionals Day

Wednesday of the Last Full Week of April

Find Skilled Help for Home and Work

Thumbtack

Freelancer Marketplace for Projects and Experts

thumbtack.com

 APRIL 7

National No Housework Day

Perhaps the best way to celebrate National No House-work Day on April 7 is to visit a handyperson marketplace to hire someone to clean for you. **Thumbtack** is the perfect place to find someone to mount your flat-screen TV, capture your next event on video, weed your garden and kick your butt in a workout.

Get a Real Human on the Phone for Customer Service

GetHuman

Reference Site for Customer Service Numbers, Shortcuts, Answers and More

gethuman.com

 APRIL 25

National Telephone Day

The first National Telephone Day (April 25) was in 1967, just after the 100 millionth telephone line was installed in the U.S. Since then we've been trying to use the dang phone to get someone at the dang customer service center to figure out why our dang cable just went out.

Skip the on-hold music and endless phone trees to find an actual human to talk to with **GetHuman**. The site lists shortcuts to contact thousands of companies to get to an actual human.

Stay Safe

Passwords and Security

Check to See If Your Email Has Been Breached

Have I Been Pwned?

Search Engine for Hacked Emails and Usernames

haveibeenpwned.com

SEPTEMBER

National IT Professionals Day

Third Tuesday of September

National IT Professionals Day is the third Tuesday of September. Do them a favor and check your passwords. At **Have I Been Pwned?** enter your emails and usernames into the search engine, and the site scans millions of records that have been released after data breaches. The site will share the name of the breach as well as when it happened and what they stole. Even if you haven't been breached, make your IT friends even happier by taking control of your passwords with the tools on Page 31.

Upgrade Your Passwords

The first Thursday in May is World Password Day. One of the most common online security mistakes we make, besides picking passwords that are too easy, is using the same password for multiple sites.

The bad guys know this, and when they hack into a site, they get our username/password combos and try them on other sites and eventually get to some pretty valuable information. It's time to truly take charge of your password and Internet security issues.

You can't go wrong with any of the top password managers, such as **1Password**, **Dashlane** and **Keeper**. I use **LastPass**, mainly because it's the one I started with. And I love that I can share passwords with staffers and contractors without letting them see the actual login info.

In 2020, LastPass made everyone mad because they limited their free version to one device. **Bitwarden** offers the free features that LastPass used to.

Quick note: It does you no good to use a password manager but still reuse passwords. Create a unique, unguessable password for every. single. site.

Really.

1Password
Top Password Manager with Offline Storage and Manual Sync
1password.com

Bitwarden
Password Manager with Generous Free Version
bitwarden.com

Dashlane
Top Password Manager with Online/Offline Storage Options
dashlane.com

Keeper
Top Password Manager with Extra Secure Security
keepersecurity.com

LastPass
Beth Z's Favorite Password Manager
lastpass.com

 MAY

World Password Day

First Thursday in May

STAY SAFE

Protect Your Computer from Malware and More

Kaspersky Security Cloud Free

Best Free Security Tool

kaspersky.com/free-cloud-antivirus

Malwarebytes Free

Adware and Malware Removal App

malwarebytes.com

NOVEMBER 30

Computer Security Day

Isn't it disgusting that we have so many words for the horrible things that bad guys dream up to muck up our computers? Jeeze. For Computer Security Day on November 30, take steps to protect your computer with these free tools.

Malware is software such as viruses, worms, Trojan horses and spyware. **Malwarebytes** has been the best free tool in this category for years. It's the one I use. I like that you can upgrade to get robust protection from ransomware, the programs that literally hold your files hostage and make you pay to get them back. For more overall protection, **Kaspersky Security Cloud Free** ranks the best.

Privacy

Learn How to Surf Safer

Safer Internet Day USA

Site with Resources for Staying Safe Online

saferinternetday.us

FEBRUARY

Safer Internet Day USA

Second Tuesday in February

The second Tuesday in February is **Safer Internet Day USA**. This makes me smile a little because it also falls on my mother's birthday, and she always thought my computer skills made me a hacker. The site has plenty of resources for adults and kids to learn about how to surf safely to protect privacy and your personal data.

Protect Your Digital Data

The National Cyber Security Alliance runs **StaySafe-Online** and manages Data Privacy Day (January 28). The site is full of stats to scare you and resources to help you protect yourself. Here are some of their best resources.

CyberSecure My Business™

Interactive, Easy-to-Understand Workshops for Small and Medium-Sized Businesses

staysafeonline.org/cybersecure-business

Cybersecurity Tip Sheets

Dozens of Downloadable Checklists and Tip Sheets for Everything from Romance Scams to Online Shopping

nerdybff.com/privacytipsheets

Manage Your Privacy Settings

Listing of Direct Links to Check Privacy Settings for Popular Devices and Online Services

nerdybff.com/privacysettings

Online Safety Basics

Straightforward Tips for Protecting Yourself, Your Family and Devices

nerdybff.com/safetybasics

StaySafeOnline

Home Base for All Your Cybersecurity Needs

staysafeonline.org

 JANUARY 28

Data Privacy Day

STAY SAFE

Increase Your Cybersecurity Smarts

Cybersecurity Awareness Month

Event to Raise Awareness about Cybersecurity so the Horrible Hackers Won't Get You

staysafeonline.org/ cybersecurity-awareness- month

OCTOBER

National Cybersecurity Awareness Month

The National Cyber Security Alliance sponsors **Cybersecurity Awareness Month** every October, in addition to Data Privacy Day in January (Page 33) and Identity Management Day on the second Tuesday in April. Check out their page to find educational resources and links to Cybersecurity Awareness Month events near you.

Ask Your Private Questions in Private

DuckDuckGo

Privacy-First Browser and Search Engine

duckduckgo.com

SEPTEMBER 28

Ask a Stupid Question Day

You can ask as many questions as you want on Ask a Stupid Question Day (September 28), but if you Google "Why do I have so much belly button lint?" the search engine is going to eventually show you ads for a Belly Button Duster (just $5.11 at Walmart in case you're interested).

You can follow the guidelines on increasing your privacy for Google searches, or you can switch to **DuckDuckGo**, a search engine and browser where privacy is the biggest concern.

🔍	why is my belly button lint
🔍	why is my belly button lint **red**
🔍	why is my belly button lint **always blue**
🔍	why is my belly button lint **black**
🔍	why is my belly button lint **blue**
🔍	why is my belly button **fluff blue**
🔍	why **does** my belly button lint **smell**
🔍	why **does** my belly button **fluff smell**
🔍	why is lint **in** my belly button
🔍	why **does** my belly button **collect** lint
🔍	why **does** my belly button **produce** lint

Robocalls and Phone Scams

Register Your Phone Number on the Do Not Call List

I feel a little pessimistic about the spam-prevention protection provided by registering on the **National Do Not Call Registry**, but since the first full week in March is National Consumer Protection Week, it's worth a shot.

The event encourages people to learn more about scams, understand their consumer rights and make better decisions about money. Check out more resources on the **Federal Trade Commission's** site, where you can report fraud, scams and identity theft.

Federal Trade Commission

Government Site with Resources to Report Identity Theft and Fraud

consumer.ftc.gov

National Do Not Call Registry

Site to Register Your Numbers to Avoid Telemarketing Calls

donotcall.gov

 MARCH

National Consumer Protection Week

First Full Week in March

STAY SAFE

Flip the Tables on Phone Scammers

Hiya
Spam Caller Blocker with Free Version and $15/Year Pro

hiya.com

Nomorobo
Award-Winning Robocall Blocker with Free VoIP Landline Service and Budget Mobile Protection

nomorobo.com

RoboKiller
Robocall and Spam Blocking Service with Spammer Revenge

robokiller.com

YouMail
Phone Spam Protection with a Smart Voicemail Solution

youmail.com

JANUARY 25

National Opposite Day

When a phone rings with an unknown number, we all fear robocallers, scammers and spammers. January 25 is National Opposite Day, a perfect opportunity to turn the scammers into the scammed. **RoboKiller** is a call management tool that seeks to engage the scammer in a time-wasting, inane conversation with a realistic recorded voice. RoboKiller answers the call for you and starts responding with a colorful collection of crazy conversations. Your scammer may be caught up in a chat with a grumpy old man, a person who just had an alien encounter or an overly gracious southern belle.

Other robocall services worth mentioning are **YouMail**, **Hiya** and **Nomorobo**. You're going to have to pay $20 to $50+ or so a year for the privilege of avoiding annoying calls and spam texts. The major phone providers (Verizon, T-Mobile, AT&T, etc.) also offer additional protection, but again, you're going to have to upgrade to get the best blockers.

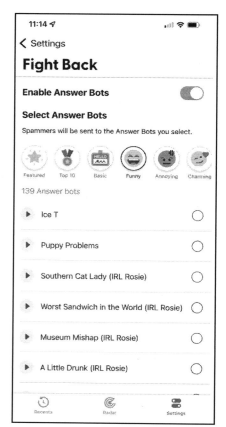

Be Efficient

Office Software

Discover Free Software

FEBRUARY

Free and Open Source Software Month

February is Free and Open Source Software Month! We nerds celebrate the programmers and developers who share their creations so that we all benefit. To celebrate, check out these free open source options that hold their own against the well-known paid versions.

Audacity
Open-Source Audio Editing Tool
audacityteam.org

GIMP
Adobe Photoshop-Like Image Editor
gimp.org

KeePass
Free Password Manager
keepass.info

LibreOffice
Microsoft Office's Free Competitor
libreoffice.org

Moodle
Free Online Learning Platform to Build Online Courses
moodle.org

Scribus
Free Desktop Publishing Tool and Microsoft Publisher Alternative
scribus.net

Find the Right Tech Tool for Your Small Business

Congress designated the third week in February as National Entrepreneurship Week to encourage American entrepreneurs and spark new businesses.

Before you buy a bunch of tech tools and start your trial-and-error software tests, check out software review sites such as **Capterra**, **G2** and **TrustRadius** for reviews from real users, software descriptions, use cases and more. Some of the most popular categories are CRMs, project management, email marketing and human resources. It's a great place to start when you're looking for something proven that will help your business and work life.

Capterra
Software Review and Selection Platform with Free Consultations
capterra.com

G2
Huge Software Review Site
g2.com

TrustRadius
Another Software Review Site
trustradius.com

FEBRUARY

National Entrepreneurship Week

Third Week in February

BE EFFICIENT

There's an App (Day) for That!

Oh app-y day! December 11 is National App Day. One of my favorite sites for new apps is **Product Hunt**, which is like the Reddit for tech tools.

All the cool kids with the cool new tech tools hang out on Product Hunt. New tools are "hunted" by the tool founder or another community member. Registered users then upvote the best tools. You can browse by category or just keep up with the day's trends. No matter how you bump around, you're going to find great web apps, cloud companies and design tools.

Product Hunt
Launchpad for New Tech Tools and Gadgets
producthunt.com

DECEMBER 11

National App Day

Upgrade Your Spreadsheets

Airtable

Super-Powered
Spreadsheet/Database Tool

airtable.com

OCTOBER 17

Spreadsheet Day

If you love a good pivot table, celebrate the anniversary of the first copy of VisiCalc, the first personal computer spreadsheet software.

Spreadsheet Day (October 17) gives us the opportunity

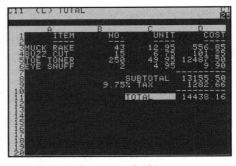

By User:Gortu - apple2history.org,
Public Domain, commons.wikimedia.org/
w/index.php?curid=342925

to upgrade the humble cell-filled file. **Airtable** is either a database tool disguised as a spreadsheet or a spreadsheet tool with database superpowers. Either way, Airtable gives you linked data tools to manage everything from personal budgets to company sales tracking.

Bring Data to Life

Flourish

Sexy Visualization Tool for
Data and Charts

flourish.studio

OCTOBER 20

**Information
Overload Day**

It's not surprising that someone created Information Overload Day (October 20). Don't contribute to the problem of information overload… make sure your information is easily understood and visible.

Google has aggregated all kinds of data and data visualization tools that will give you charts and graphs far more exciting than Microsoft Excel's 3D pie chart. They can be colorful, animated, interactive and engaging — a great way to bring your boring statistics to life. Many of the databases and visualization tools are available in the Journalist Studio (Page 134). The site **Flourish** is by far my favorite.

Email Tools

Work Toward Inbox Zero

The last business week in January is Clean Out Your Inbox Week. If you prefer texting to answering emails, try the conversational email tool **Spike** to make an email thread look like a texting conversation. Or try **SaneBox** for AI-powered email triage. **Spark** is another helper-email tool, and it's extra good for teams.

SaneBox
AI-Powered Email Triage App
sanebox.com

Spark
Intelligent Email Tool that Works Well with Teams
sparkmailapp.com

Spike
Conversational Email Tool with Collaboration Features
spikenow.com

JANUARY

Clean Out Your Inbox Week

Last Business Week in January

Manage Your Inbox with Snooze Features

FollowUpThen

Email Reminder and
Management Tool

followupthen.com

 SEPTEMBER 6

**Fight
Procrastination Day**

This book is full of tools to help you celebrate Fight Procrastination Day on September 6, everything from top task-list tools (Page 11) to keeping track of your time (Page 23). Sometimes your problem is not procrastination… it's just not having enough time in the day to get things done.

Professionals spend about three hours a day mucking around in email. One way to clear out your inbox is to make use of the snooze feature in Outlook and Gmail or whatever email tool you're using. I prefer a service called **FollowUpThen**. When I have an email in my inbox that I don't need to deal with right away, I can simply forward it to an email address like

"twoweeks@followupthen.com" or

"Friday@followupthen.com"

or any other time period that I need to snooze the email. At the appointed time, the email comes back, and I can either deal with it or snooze it again. The service has lots of little features (paid and free) that let you create tasks, wait for responses, get regular reminders and more. You can even remind everyone on an email string by CCing your @followupthen.com address in an exchange.

Go Through Your Virtual Junk Drawers One More Time

During spring cleaning this year, you organized your email inbox and cleaned out all the unwanted subscriptions. But the day after Labor Day is National Another Look Unlimited Day, and it's the perfect opportunity to sweep through your emails to see what you can delete, organize, archive and unsubscribe from.

Unroll.me is a great way to get your subscriptions under control. You sign up via Gmail, Yahoo, Outlook or your other email providers. Then Unroll.me sweeps through your inbox to find subscriptions. The next step is to unsubscribe or convert into a daily digest with just a few clicks.

Unroll.me is now a part of NielsenIQ along with Slice, a package-tracking tool (Page 14). They are both free services that pay for themselves by aggregating data from your purchases to sell to advertising companies, answering questions such as "does free shipping drive sales?" and "how many iPhones were sold this month." I've always been fine trading some of my buying habits for these handy tools, but they've been in hot water for a lack of transparency in the past. The good news is you can now opt out of some of their data mining.

If Unroll.me makes you nervous, try a couple of paid options such as **Leave Me Alone** and **Clean Email**.

Clean Email

Email Manager with Unsubscribe Services

clean.email

Leave Me Alone

Email Spam and Subscription Manager

leavemealone.app

Unroll.me

Free Email Subscription Manager, Now with More Privacy

unroll.me

 SEPTEMBER

National Another Look Unlimited Day

Day after Labor Day

Use Disposable Email Addresses to Protect Your Privacy

10 Minute Mail
Disposable Emails that Disappear after 10 Minutes
10minutemail.com

Apple's Hide My Email Feature
Apple's iCloud-Based Email Masking Feature
On iOS Devices

Burner Mail
Masked Email Address Generator for Privacy and Spam Protection
burnermail.io

Email on Deck
Temporary Emails for Privacy and Spam Protection
emailondeck.com

Gmail Email Privacy Hack
Gmail Feature to Let You Mask Your Email Address with a Plus Sign and Word or Phrase
Gmail Feature

Mailinator
Disposable Email Addresses on the Go
mailinator.com

 OCTOBER 13

International Skeptics Day

When it comes to sites that ask you to enter your email address, we should all recognize International Skeptics Day on October 13. By using masked or temporary email addresses on unknown sites, you're putting a buffer between your inbox and potential scams, spam or just relentless marketers.

Both **Gmail** and **Apple Mail** have email tricks to mask your real address. With Gmail, just modify your regular Gmail address with a plus sign and another word, such as "bethz+newsletterlist@gmail.com." Apple Mail will generate one for you as well.

I've used **Burner Mail** for many years. The Chrome extension generates unique email addresses for new sites, and I can turn off the email address if needed to protect my privacy and my inbox. **Email on Deck** is another great tool for an email address you need just long enough to get the download you just signed up for. Just visit the website and prove that you're human to get a random address that lasts about 10 minutes.

And speaking of 10 minutes, another quick site is **10 Minute Mail**. As soon as you get to the site, you'll see a unique address that will last for (you guessed it) 10 minutes. Finally, tools like **Mailinator** let you make up an email address on the fly then retrieve your message on their site. The downside of Mailinator is that your made-up email address is not unique and not secure, so anything you send there can be seen by others.

File Management

Convert Your Files to a New Format

The last day of January is National Backward Day, and since **Zamzar** can convert files backwards and forwards, it's the perfect time to include it.

This is my seventh technology book, and Zamzar has been in every one. I searched high and low for a better conversion tool, but I'm still in love. Why mess with the best?

Visit the site, upload a file, choose what you want to turn it into and press a button. In a matter of minutes, your file is transformed into the format you need.

Wait, there's more! You can convert files via email as well, just by writing to [format]@zamzar.com. For example, you can send your Microsoft Word file to pdf@zamzar.com. In a few minutes, you'll receive a link to your new pdf. Or you can send your PDF to doc@zamzar.com, and the opposite happens. It's magic either way.

Zamzar

File Converter Extraordinaire

zamzar.com

 JANUARY 31

National Backward Day

Share Files from One Device to Another

On National Do a Grouch a Favor Day (February 16), you have the opportunity to make a grumpy coworker's life easier and bring a smile. When they need the video from the holiday party that you have on your phone, head to **Snapdrop**, a site that lets you transfer files from one device to another in seconds.

Snapdrop

Online Service to Transfer Files Between Devices

snapdrop.net

 FEBRUARY 16

National Do a Grouch a Favor Day

Back Up Your Computer and Files

World Backup Day Pledge

Site with Simple Tips for Backing Up Your Files

worldbackupday.com

 MARCH 31

World Backup Day

The last day of March is yet another important date in the world of cybersecurity. **World Backup Day** on March 31 encourages you to, believe it or not, back up. Their motto: "friends don't let friends go without a backup." Take the pledge to back up your files and spread the word on their site.

Back Up Your Computer and Files (continued)

Cloud storage tools like Dropbox are great for storing documents for easy access and safekeeping in case your hard drive dies. But they're not really designed to back up your computer. You want a tool that not only saves and syncs your file but also replicates your computer's software innards so you can rebuild the whole machine.

The most robust backup tool has a bucket of features that overlap with cloud storage tools as well as cybersecurity safeguards. That's probably why they call it **Acronis Cyber Protect Home Office**. Another backup favorite with a free version is **Paragon Backup & Recovery**.

Third-party backup tools are smart, but sometimes it's a pain to install and maintain yet another tool to just run your everyday computing needs. Both Mac and Windows platforms come with built-in backup systems that you just need to enable. I use **Time Machine** on my Mac with an external hard drive. And you can enable **Backup and Restore** in settings on Windows machines to automatically keep copies of your system in case the worst happens.

Acronis Cyber Protect Home Office

Super-Secure Backup System with Ransomware Protection

acronis.com

Microsoft Backup and Restore

Microsoft's Built-In Backup Tool

nerdybff.com/windowsbackup

Paragon Backup & Recovery

Cloud Backup Tool with Free Level for Non-Commercial Use

paragon-software.com

Time Machine

Mac's Built-In Backup Tool

nerdybff.com/timemachine

Find Your Duplicate Files

Duplicate Cleaner for Windows

Windows Duplicate File Finder

digitalvolcano.co.uk/ duplicatecleaner.html

Gemini 2

Mac Duplicate File Finder

macpaw.com/gemini

APRIL 20

National Look Alike Day

National Look Alike Day (April 20) is great for celebrating doppelgangers, but duplicate files and photos on your computers and phones aren't as fun. Spend the day searching and organizing your devices for duplicate files that take up space and resources. **Duplicate Cleaner for Windows** has a robust free version that lets you find and manage documents, photos, music and other files that are scattered in different folders. On Macs, I use **Gemini** to root out the excess copies.

Stop the Frantic Searches for the Files You Need for Today's Meeting

Searchable.ai

Multi-App Search Engine to Find Files, Emails, Chats and More No Matter Where They Live

searchable.ai

JUNE 18

International Panic Day

International Panic Day (June 18) was founded to remind people to stop the stress and get more perspective. Many people do experience crippling panic attacks, and many more are familiar with the heart-racing scramble that happens when we're unprepared.

Reduce stress and increase efficiency by using universal search tools such as **Searchable.ai** to look for files, replies, chat conversations and more at the same time. Then you don't have to hunt through each area individually.

Utilities

Discover If a Website Is Down

When Anne Moeller's alarm didn't go off on a Friday the 13th in 1982, she suffered a series of bad luck incidents, so she proclaimed the first Friday the 13th of every year as Blame Someone Else Day.

When you pull up a website for a presentation, and it won't load, you can check to see if you can blame someone else. The cleverly named **Down for Everyone or Just Me?** site lets you paste in a troublesome link to find out if it's, well, down for everyone or just you.

Another good resource is **Down Detector**, which checks services such as cable services, phone companies, streaming platforms, video game networks and social media sites.

Down Detector

Real-Time Problem and Outage Monitoring

downdetector.com

Down for Everyone or Just Me?

Site that Checks to See If Websites Are Down

downforeveryoneorjustme.com

📅 **VARIOUS**

National Blame Someone Else Day

First Friday the 13th of Every Year

Autofill Your Cookie Consent

Super Agent

Browser Extension to
Opt Out of Website
Cookies Automatically

super-agent.com

 OCTOBER

**National
Cookie Month**

Sooo many celebrations revolve around cookies. There's National Cookie Month in October, plus recognition for traditional cookies such as National Chocolate Cookie Day (August 4), National Sugar Cookie Day (July 9) and National Peanut Butter Cookie Day (June 12). The holidays also get fancy and oddly specific like Lacy Oatmeal Cookie Day (March 18) and National Pfeffernusse Day (December 23). You also have cookie preparation recognition like National Cookie Cutter Week (the first week of December) and Gingerbread Decorating Day (December 12).

We may love the baked cookies, but no one likes an obnoxious cookie consent form, the popup boxes on websites that give sites permission to track you. The European Union's General Data Protection Regulation (GDPR) requires that visitors must be notified of data that sites are collecting and get permission from them to collect it. We put one on yournerdybestfriend.com just in case. But that doesn't mean we like them.

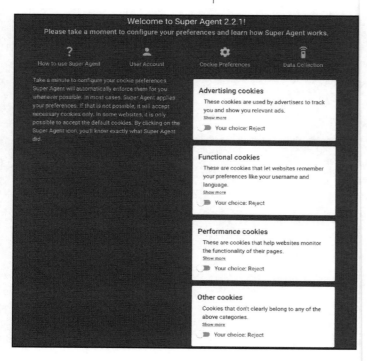

The browser extension **Super Agent** removes the need to click that dang box because it does the work for you. You can tell it you want to opt out of cookies such as advertising and performance. Because I always take the time to opt out of optional cookies, Super Agent is a real time saver.

Check Your Internet Speed

The beloved sitcom "I Love Lucy" premiered on October 15, 1951. Before you binge your favorite episodes on National I Love Lucy Day, make sure your internet connection can handle it. Go to Netflix's **Fast.com** website to see instant stats on your internet upload and download speeds.

Fast.com

Internet Speed Checking Site

fast.com

 OCTOBER 15

**National
I Love Lucy Day**

Get All Your Computer Details Instantly

The IT professionals in your office totally deserve your thanks on the last Friday of July: System Administrator Appreciation Day.

Make their lives easier when they ask you for details like your operating system, browser and more. Just go to the site called **Support Details**, and your, uh, support details will show up on the screen with all the info your technical support team will ask.

Support Details

Site to Detect Computer Settings and More

supportdetails.com

 JULY

**System
Administrator
Appreciation Day**

Last Friday of July

Send a Free Fax Online

FaxZero

Free Online Fax Tool

faxzero.com

 MARCH 10

National Landline Telephone Day

I bet you know very few people who still have a land-line… and even fewer people who still fax stuff. But because there are still people who celebrate National Landline Telephone Day (March 10), we still need to know how to fax things if needed.

FaxZero lets you fax for free from your computer in seconds. Don't send anything private unless you upgrade a few bucks to send with more privacy.

Communicate Clearly

COMMUNICATE

Writing

Let Artificial Intelligence Write for You

Jarvis

AI Writing Tool with Templates and Open Writing Tools

jarvis.ai

Rytr

Bargain-Priced AI Writing Tool

rytr.me

Writecream

AI Writing Tool that Generates Audio and Images

writecream.com

 MARCH

Words Matter Week

First Full Week of March

I have a master's degree in journalism, and writing has always been pretty easy for me. But many people struggle with finding the right words, creating copy and communicating their points clearly. The first full week of March, celebrate Words Matter Week with the National Association of Independent Writers and Editors. Now's the time to try out a mind-blowing technology that will help unstick your writer's block: AI writing assistants.

AI writing tools exploded in number in 2021 thanks to a new AI platform that specializes in natural language processing. Just write a few bullet points about your subject, and the AI tools will generate copy for your rough draft. Most tools have templates to help you with cold emails, Instagram captions, blog posts and more. Other tools let you instruct the AI in a more conversational tone, such as, "Write an outline for a blog post about how to block distractions."

Jarvis is my first AI writing tool love. I actually visited the company in person to understand their technology and roadmap. **Rytr** is a very reasonable alternative with great functionality. Another one called **Writecream** will even create images and audio "icebreakers" for your outreach.

Fix ~~You're~~ Your Grammar

March 4 is National Grammar Day, and National Proofreading Day is March 8. Many software platforms have integrated artificial intelligence tools to check your grammar and spelling while you work, but **Grammarly** has improved immensely since it started and is still one of the best. The **Hemingway App** site also provides valuable feedback for better copy.

Grammarly
AI-Powered Grammar Checker
grammarly.com

Hemingway App
Online Writing Coach and Grammar Checker
hemingwayapp.com

 MARCH 4
National Grammar Day

 MARCH 8
National Proofreading Day

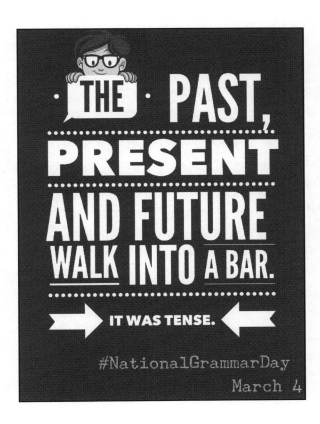

COMMUNICATE

Revel in Rhymes and Play with Words

Rhymezone

Search Engine for Rhyming Words, Phrases and More

rhymezone.com

JANUARY 9

National Word Nerd Day

I used to read the dictionary for fun, and my newsletter is called NerdWords. So National Word Nerd Day (January 9) makes my logophilic heart sing.

Rhymezone is more than a resource for finding sound-alike words for your songwriting. It helps with finding similar sounding words for business names, program titles and other phrases that need a musical quality. And it's just so much fun!

Compose on an Old-Fashioned Typewriter

Hanx Writer

Tom Hanks' iPad App that Simulates a Typewriter

In the App Store

Typewrite Something

Online Typewriter Simulator

typewritesomething.com

JUNE 23

National Typewriter Day

June 23 is National Typewriter Day, when American inventor Christopher Latham Sholes received approval for the typewriter patent in 1868.

Actor Tom Hanks loves vintage typewriters and even helped develop **Hanx Writer**, an iPad app that simulates writing on a typewriter (still works but hasn't been updated in years). If you aren't an Apple person, just go to **Typewrite Something** for the clickety-clack of a vintage machine.

Have an Awesome, Stupendous, Magnificent Day

Thesaurus pioneer Peter Mark Roget was born January 18, 1779. Celebrate National Thesaurus Day by visualizing word connections with **Visuwords** and looking up words in dozens of dictionaries at the same time with the ultimate dictionary search tool, **OneLook**.

OneLook

Dictionary Search Engine that Looks up Words and Phrases in Multiple Dictionaries at Once

onelook.com

Visuwords

Site that Shows Relationships to Words

visuwords.com

JANUARY 18

National Thesaurus Day

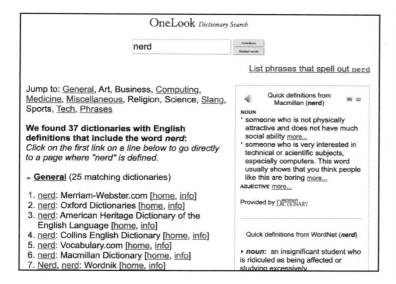

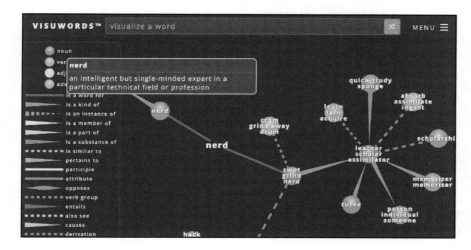

Connecting

Reach Out in the New Year

Felt

Accordion-Style Greeting
Card from Your Phone

feltapp.com

Punkpost

Artistic Cards from Real Artists

punkpost.com

JANUARY

**Universal Letter
Writing Week**

Second Full Week
of January

The second full week of January is Universal Letter Writing Week. These snail mail apps will help you reach out without lifting a pen or finding a stamp.

For $6 a month, you can send up to three four-paneled **Felt** cards (including U.S. shipping). I use them for everything from a client thank-you to a husband I-love-you. And on **Punkpost** for starting at $7 a card, you can send handwritten notes from real artists just by typing your message and adding an address.

Personalize Your Communication

According to a 2020 Adobe survey of marketers and consumers, creating a personalized experience for customers increases loyalty, revenue and retention. This is good to keep in mind for Get to Know Your Customers Days: the third Thursdays in January, April, July and October.

Take time to set up some personalization with a crazy tool called **WOXO**. The video generator lets you batch produce videos for social media and marketing by using a spreadsheet. Each video can have a different name, a different greeting, a different product highlight, a different soundtrack... you name it. And when you push the button to render them, poof! You get a pile of personalized videos to share with each contact.

You can also set up a dynamic video template. The video has placeholders for the personalized areas. Then the data can be inserted just by adding words into each URL. When the contact clicks on the unique URL, they'll see their name or whatever in the video template.

WOXO

Tool to Produce Personalized Videos with the Push of a Button.

woxo.tech

 VARIOUS

Get to Know Your Customers Day

Every Third Thursday in January, April, July and October

COMMUNICATE

Write a Better Email

Boomerang

Email Taming and Tracking Tool with AI-Powered Writing Help

boomerangapp.com

 JUNE

National Business Etiquette Week

First Full Week of June

Have you ever re-read a sent email and cringed because it came off as snippy? Sometimes when we're plowing through the day's inbox, we lose perspective. Email wrangler **Boomerang** has an AI-powered writing coach that analyzes the tone and temperature of your emails before you hit send. It's just the type of feature that will get you through National Business Etiquette Week the first full week of June.

Boomerang also helps you track sent emails, pauses your inbox when you need to be productive, reminds you when you haven't heard from someone and generally helps you be more email efficient. It integrates with Gmail and Outlook and also has a stand-alone mobile app.

Write Your Thank You Notes

Calligraphr

Site to Create Your Own Handwritten Fonts

calligraphr.com

 DECEMBER 26

National Thank You Note Day

The day after Christmas is National Thank You Note Day, which makes me feel bad for all the thanks I haven't sent from last year's gifts.

Handwritten notes are the best, but if you have a LOT of cards to write, consider making your own font. **Calligraphr** lets you create a font in your handwriting or any style you like. Then you can download it and use it like any other font on your computer.

Collaboration

Organize Your Meetings to Save Time and Stress

A 2021 survey found that 94 percent of employees feel happier when they can take a lunch break, but 40 percent said they only occasionally, rarely or never take breaks during the workday (for women it was 67 percent!). And since one of the biggest timewasters in the office is mindless meetings, try an app that organizes agendas and keeps track of all the meeting discussions and decisions. Next thing you know, you'll have extra time to free up the third Friday in June so you can celebrate National Take Back the Lunch Break Day.

Sesh, which seems extra cool because it's short for "session," is my favorite. You can create agendas, keep track of tasks, conduct structured brainstorming and take notes, etc. Sesh was one of the first to partner with Zoom in the Zoom App Marketplace. This links the agenda to the video call and even keeps track of who is speaking and how long they speak.

Other cool features are the icebreaker templates and even scheduled focus time.

Hugo is another cool new agenda tool with meeting and schedule management.

Hugo
Meeting and Schedule
Management Tool
hugo.team

Sesh
Meeting Agenda
Tool Integrated into
Zoom Meetings
sesh.com

 JUNE

**National Take Back
the Lunch Break Day**

Third Friday in June

COMMUNICATE

Celebrate (and Corral) Your Volunteers

SignUp.com
Sign Up Sheet and Volunteer Organization Site
signup.com

SignUpGenius
Volunteer Organizer Tool
signupgenius.com

 FEBRUARY

International Optimist Day

First Thursday in February

Optimist Day sounds pretty self-explanatory… always look on the bright side of life, right? But it's actually an official celebration for members of Optimist International, which is made up of clubs that "participate in community service programs that are dedicated to bringing out the best in youth."

Luckily the Optimist Clubs are happy to share International Optimist Day on the first Thursday in February. They encourage us to celebrate by volunteering and spreading optimistic messages.

If you're volunteering, you are dealing with other volunteers. Check out **SignUp.com** and **SignUpGenius** for free tools to organize and track your volunteers.

Collaborate Better with Long-Distance Colleagues

A new trend in office tech tools is perfect for celebrating National Work from Home Day on the last Thursday in June. To use them, you need to shift your mindset from thinking about files and folders to embracing workspaces and whiteboards.

Another newcomer to the collaboration competition is **ClickUp**, which bills itself as "one app to replace them all." With a free-forever level, ClickUp is a great place to start for a simple collaboration home base.

Monday.com and **Notion** are online hubs for remote workers. They replace the idea of emails sent to individuals and files kept in individual folders. With the new workplace tools, everyone's tasks, projects, files and research are all shared in one workspace (with options to keep areas private, of course). The shift is more collaborative and open rather than siloed and separate.

ClickUp

Workflow and Workplace App "to Replace Them All"

clickup.com

Monday.com

Hub for Project Management, Tasks, Documents and More

monday.com

Notion

Workspace for Notes, Tasks, Life

notion.so

 JUNE

National Work from Home Day

Last Thursday in June

COMMUNICATE

Manage Your Projects

Trello

Project Management Tool Good for Personal Task Management

trello.com

 NOVEMBER

International Project Management Day

First Thursday in November

The project management world is a crowded space, but a few companies stand out and are worthy of celebration on the first Thursday in November, aka International Project Management Day. These tools are the most recommended by audience members in my sessions, and those folks are way smarter than I am.

You'll find many of the same characteristics in the top contenders. In general, here are the features these tools contain:

- Capability to set up projects with tasks, goals and milestones
- Collaboration tools for teams
- Feeds and dashboards for latest activity and status updates
- Ability to assign tasks to team members
- Shareable file library
- Notification system via email or third-party tools
- Multi-device access to cloud-based data
- Free or low-cost basic features with upgrades for larger teams and projects

Beyond these common characteristics, you'll find variety in the look and feel of the most popular tools.

Trello offers an interesting take on project management by organizing your projects into "cards" that lay out like a deck across your screen. You can click on any card to flip it over and see the details, including tasks, collaborators and due dates.

Manage Your Projects (continued)

Trello organizes all your projects into boards, allowing both personal and shared boards. Your account lets you have as many boards as you want, and you can manage the permissions for each for everything from read-only access to full privileges. You create lists and deadlines for each board, and you can assign tasks to others. It's easy to reprioritize and assign list items with a quick click and drag.

Asana and **Smartsheet** are crowd favorites at my sessions. Many teams report that Asana gives small teams everything they need at no cost for up to 15 users. And although Smartsheet isn't free, its users adore the fact that the system has templates for almost any type of project, and the layout is the familiar spreadsheet format.

Basecamp was probably the first online project management system, and it's undoubtedly one of the most popular. Basecamp also has the most integrations, including social networks, mobile phones and invoicing software. All the systems update each other and keep everyone on track. They have a limited free version, or an all-in flat rate of $99 for unlimited. Teachers and students get free accounts.

If you want the basic structure of Basecamp without the $99 a month, try **Freedcamp.** Unlimited users. Unlimited projects. Unlimited storage. What's not to love? Freedcamp gives away much more than many of the other top project management systems in this section. They start charging for integrations with Google Drive, larger file uploads, CRMs, invoices and issue tracking.

Asana
Favorite Project Management Tool with Robust Free Version
asana.com

Basecamp
Classic Project Management System
basecamp.com

Freedcamp
Mostly Free Project Management System
freedcamp.com

Smartsheet
Spreadsheet-Based Project Management Tool
smartsheet.com

COMMUNICATE

Contact Management

Expand Your Professional Circles

Contacts+

Contact Management System with Intelligent De-Duping and Updates

contactsplus.com

FEBRUARY

International Networking Week

First Week in February

Of course you want to network to celebrate International Networking Week the first week of February. But if your contact list is a mess, you'll never be able to find your new connections again.

Every time I have a discussion with attendees about contact management systems, **Contacts+** is the top response. The system merges your duplicate contacts, even from different devices and platforms, keeping all your contact systems current no matter where they live. It also scans public data to keep you up to date with your contacts' latest photos, jobs and social profiles. When your contacts have a new signature line, Contacts+ updates the info in their profile.

Clean Up Your Contacts List

Cloze

Contact Manager Tool for Relationship Management

cloze.com

NOVEMBER 17

National Unfriend Day

Don't be the person with whom your contact celebrates National Unfriend Day on November 17! **Cloze** is a contact management tool that links social media to help you keep up with your contacts and keep an eye on their social media accounts. The paid version has even more CRM-type features such as tracking texts, emails and more.

Remember People's Names

Reaching out to make a new connection can be challenging, but it's even more challenging when you make a new friend then forget their name. Celebrate National Make a Friend Day on February 11 by downloading **Rememorate**, an app that helps you learn the names and details about your connections.

Rememorate

Contact Management Tool that Helps You Remember Names

rememorate.com

 FEBRUARY 11

National Make a Friend Day

Find Out What Makes Your Contacts Tick

The Monday after Labor Day is National Boss/Employee Exchange Day. This sounds like a great idea on paper, but what if your boss is a mystery to you? Once upon a time, I had a real job. I liked my boss personally, but professionally I just felt like he and I were on different planets. And, according to a creepy tool called **Crystal**, he and I were as well matched as Michael Scott and Toby Flenderson from "The Office."

Crystal uses artificial intelligence to analyze people's social media presence and any correspondence you've exchanged. Then it puts your connection into a personality profile to give you insights on their motivations, communication preferences, personality traits and more.

Yes, it is a step too far, and that's why I call it #HelpfulButCreepy.

Crystal

Contact Research Tool that Analyzes Personalities

crystalknows.com

 SEPTEMBER

National Boss/Employee Exchange Day

Monday after Labor Day

COMMUNICATE

Figure Out Where Your Contacts Hang

Batch GEO

Lead Mapping Tool

batchgeo.com

Google My Maps

Another Lead Mapping Tool

google.com/mymaps

 JULY 1

Zip Code Day

Zip Code Day on July 1 is the perfect opportunity to visualize your contact base. Both **BatchGeo** and **Google My Maps** let you upload spreadsheets of your prospects or clients to see where they are and where they're not, giving you great insight into where you should focus your sales and marketing efforts. BatchGeo has some advanced features with the paid level, but Google My Maps is free, so….

Find Emails for New Connections

Hunter

Research Tool that Discovers Email Addresses from Domains

hunter.io

 FEBRUARY 27

No Brainer Day

To celebrate No Brainer Day on February 27, let a handy site help you figure out company emails without any effort.

Let's say you'd like to find someone at my company. You'd go to **Hunter** and enter my URL, and every publicly listed email address for people at our company will show up along with the source of the info. You can also verify email addresses and search a couple of different ways, including with browser extensions. You get 50 searches a month for free. Hunter also has a mail merge feature called Campaigns for bulk emailing and tracking. It's like a little secret mail merge site for your cold emails with systems for tracking whether they have opened, responded, called the cops, etc.

Meet Better

MEET BETTER

Online Meeting Tools

Host Asynchronous Meetings

Comeet

Asynchronous Meeting Tool

comeet.me

 SEPTEMBER 5

National Be Late for Something Day

Sure, you could celebrate National Be Late for Something Day on September 5 by purposefully logging on slowly to your next online meeting. But wouldn't getting rid of some of those meetings be more efficient? Try tools like **Comeet** to create asynchronous meetings. You have an agenda and goals as usual, but instead of finding a time to meet, you and your colleagues create a thread of short responses and videos. The meeting takes place, but it's at everyone's convenience, rather than scheduled into a block of time that took two weeks to coordinate.

Put a Little Zip in Your Zoom

I don't think the founders of Telecommuter Appreciation Week could have anticipated its worldwide adoption. The date is a tribute to telephone pioneer Alexander Graham Bell because it's always the week of his birthday (March 3).

Since much of the working world experienced telecommuting in 2020, many millions of people learned to say "you're on mute" on cue. **Zoom** became the breakout star of the online meeting world, and they continue to innovate faster than anyone else.

Zoom is always adding features, and you'll be the coolest kid in the Zoom block party if you learn the new tricks first. Keep your software updated (easier now that you can automate updates) and drop by the Zoom blog now and then to see what's new.

A fun fact about Alexander Graham Bell: In 2013 scientists rescued the first recording of Bell's voice from an ancient disc. And of course they put it online.

nerdybff.com/bell

Zoom

The Videoconference Tool that Became a Verb

zoom.com

 MARCH

Telecommuter Appreciation Week

First Week in March

MEET BETTER

Try an Online Video Tool that Isn't Zoom

Around

Conversational (and Cute) Online Meeting and Hanging Out Tool

around.co

NOVEMBER 3

Cliché Day

According to Dictionary.com, a cliché is "an expression, idea, or action that has been overused to the point of seeming worn out, stale, ineffective, or meaningless." I'm not trying to say that Zoom online meetings are a way to celebrate Cliché Day on November 3, but no one ever created the phrase "Skype fatigue." Take a break from your regular Zoom Hollywood Squares to try another online meeting tool. **Around** is made for co-working with small groups for more meaningful and colorful online meetings.

See Your Connections Face to Face

mmhmm

Zoom Alternative with Creative Graphic Interface and Fun Personality

mmhmm.app

OOO

Video Meeting Tool with Creative Backgrounds and Fun Interface

ooo.mmhmm.app

DECEMBER 28

National Call a Friend Day

Since National Call a Friend Day is December 28 when most of your contacts are probably off for the holidays, wait until the new year to invite your connections to a non-Zoom face-to-face meeting. The founder of Evernote created a (fun and funny) video conferencing tool called **mmhmm** because they like "names that you can say while eating." The app has personality and lets you showcase your slides and graphics without your head being small and the slides being rectangular. The company also released another fun video meeting alternative called **OOO**. You gotta love that. Plus… as of the end of 2021, the web version of OOO includes the warning "Dangerously Untested Preview." Gotta love that, too.

Use an AI Helper to Take Notes for You

The National Day of Listening the day after Thanksgiving reminds us to focus on our conversation partners instead of our own thoughts or our phones. Tools like **Perfect Recall** can help you focus on online conversations during Zoom calls because the service sends an AI-powered attendee to join you in the call. Perfect Recall records the meeting and allows you to add notes directly to the live transcript as the meeting happens. Then you can clip important moments in video segments to share relevant parts or repost on social media.

Perfect Recall

Zoom Meeting Recorder with Live Transcript, Note-Taking and Video Highlights

perfectrecall.app

 NOVEMBER

National Day of Listening

Day after Thanksgiving

Meeting Engagement

Start Your Next Zoom Meeting with an Icebreaker

Zoom Apps

Marketplace of Fun and Functional Apps that Integrate with Zoom

nerdybff.com/zoomapps

 JANUARY /APRIL

National Fun at Work Day

Last Friday in January or April 1

As January ends, offices should celebrate National Fun at Work Day (last Friday in January — or some celebrate it April 1). **Zoom**, everyone's favorite online meeting tool, includes integrated get-to-know-you games and add-ons in its App Marketplace.

Zoom Apps include icebreaking tools such as Heads Up! from Ellen DeGeneres, Bingo, Trivia and word-guessing games. There's even a dice game that promises "hours of multiplayer fun!"

Host a Scavenger Hunt

GooseChase

Scavenger Hunt Tool for Team Bonding in Person or Online

goosechase.com

 MAY 24

National Scavenger Hunt Day

Scavenger hunts are fun for friends and family and great at work for strengthening teams. Since May 24 is National Scavenger Hunt Day, download the **GooseChase** app and plan your own. GooseChase has free options for small groups or really big packages for really big events.

Add More Fun to Your Online Meetings

I haven't played bingo in person in… decades? But I do enjoy a fun game during an online event. For National Bingo Day on June 27, visit the wealth of engagement tools at **Flippity**. You can make your own bingo cards to print out or let people access digitally… they all get a unique card! You can also create a scavenger hunt, set up word games, create flash cards and much more with this amazing site that was made for teachers. There's even a Jeopardy-like board.

The tools are all built in Google Sheets, and they're all free. You just copy the spreadsheets and customize.

Flippity
Engagement Tools for Meetings and More
flippity.net

 JUNE 27

National Bingo Day

Share Images with Guests at an Event

Woohoo! April 3 is World Party Day. Time to get the gang together for fun, food and lots of photos. Let your fellow partiers help you create a guests-only photo album with photo-sharing tools such as **LiveShare**. Your attendees don't have to download a separate app to add photos, which is a huge help when it comes to participation.

LiveShare
Photo-Sharing Tool for Events
livesharenow.com

 APRIL 3

World Party Day

Presentations and Training

Create a How-To

Scribe

Screen Recorder that Automatically Generates Step-By-Step Guides as You Click

scribehow.com

Tango

Screen Recorder Chrome Extension for Step-By-Step Guides

tango.us

VARIABLE

Education and Sharing Day

March or April Depending on the Hebrew Calendar

Because of Rabbi Menachem Mendel Schneerson's dedication to education for all, President Jimmy Carter established the rabbi's birthday as Education and Sharing Day. It's celebrated in March or April depending on the Hebrew Calendar.

This is your opportunity to pass along knowledge using **Tango** or **Scribe**, two Chrome Extensions that record every click to create a step-by-step how to.

Both apps take screenshots as you demonstrate things like how to login to a system, how to use a web app or even "How to look 10 years younger on Zoom" in 10 easy steps.

Hire an AI Speech Coach

I've been a professional speaker for more than a decade, yet I've never taken a speech or debate class. Don't be like me! We could all use new presentation techniques to celebrate National Speech and Debate Education Day on the first Friday of March. Upgrade your speaking skills with the **Orai** app, a virtual speaking coach that will help you monitor your filler words, energy levels, clarity and more.

Orai
AI Speech Coach App
orai.com

 MARCH

National Speech and Debate Education Day

First Friday of March

Become a Better Presenter

Glossophobia, the fear of public speaking, rates higher than fear of death, spiders or heights. National Face Your Fears Day (the second Tuesday of October) is as good a time as any to address your worries about speaking in front of an audience.

If you've ever been uncomfortable while giving presentations, you're going to love a hidden feature in PowerPoint: **Rehearse with Coach**.

Go to the Slide Show menu in an updated version of Power-Point, and you'll find a button called Rehearse with Coach. When you click it, an extra box appears over your Power-Point slides. As you present, it listens to your tone, filler words, inclusive language and overall style. Then you'll get a report card and suggestions for improvement.

Rehearse with Coach
PowerPoint Feature for Real-Time Feedback on Presentations Skills
nerdybff.com/rehearsewithcoach

 OCTOBER

National Face Your Fears Day

Second Tuesday in October

Nail Your Speech in One Take with a Free Teleprompter

Teleprompter Mirror

Free Online Teleprompter with Auto Scroll or Audio-Based Advancement

telepromptermirror.com/voice-activated-teleprompter

 AUGUST 7

Professional Speakers Day

I'm a proud Certified Speaking Professional with the National Speakers Association, and I hang out with speakers all the time. So I'm sad that I haven't partied with my friends to celebrate Professional Speakers Day (August 7).

If you record video to share, using a teleprompter can help you stay on track and sound more professional. The **Teleprompter Mirror** site has a phenomenal free online teleprompter. Paste your text into the site, then choose whether the text automatically scrolls at an even pace or advances as you speak by listening through your microphone.

Think Bigger

Resumes and Careers

Upgrade Your Resume and Get Noticed

Jobscan
Resume Review Site with Job Suggestions
jobscan.co

LiveCareer
Robust Resume Checker, Cover Letter Creator and Job Tracker for about $3 a Month
livecareer.com

 NOVEMBER

Job Action Day

First Monday in November

Get your resumes in order for Job Action Day, the First Monday in November. Almost all big companies and many SMBs use an applicant tracking system (ATS) to manage and review incoming resumes.

The applicant tracking systems use artificial intelligence to evaluate and categorize your skills, qualifications, education and more. The best free resume checkers let you upload your resume and paste the job description to help you tailor your pitch to the company's needs. They look for keywords, educational requirements, job title matches and experience levels and tell you whether the ATS will judge you as a good candidate. The free versions reveal basic comparisons, and a paid level may walk you through revisions and tailoring tips. Some will even give you insights about the company's hiring software and habits.

Jobscan has a wealth of resources and free scans. Pricing starts at about $50 a month for extra features. **LiveCareer's** upgrade is less than $3, so I couldn't resist upgrading. This site has lots of resources to improve your resume and organize your job search, and it was my favorite tool overall. You can also install a Chrome Extension that helps you apply for jobs on sites like Indeed.com without having to return to LiveCareer for your resume. It also guides you through a cover letter, even prompting you to explain gaps in your resume and ending with a call to action.

Create a Home Base for All of Your Links

What secret skills do you have to unveil on November 24 for Celebrate Your Unique Talent Day? Don't keep the many sides of your life hidden anymore. **Linktree** is the mini-bio website that all the cool kids and influencers are using. Set up a page and link to all your social media profiles, side hustles, updated resume and LinkedIn account.

Linktree

Bio Link Tool for All Your Social Media Links and More

linktr.ee

 NOVEMBER 24

Celebrate Your Unique Talent Day

Capture Testimonials

The first full week of May is Update Your References Week. One of my favorite survey tools, **Typeform**, created a clever platform that lets you record a brief video of yourself asking something (it is called **videoask**, of course). Then you can encourage feedback from your viewer and ask for video responses such as testimonials. Free for 20 minutes of video a month.

Typeform

Super-Duper Survey Tool with Conversational Style

typeform.com

videoask

Video Communication Tool and Testimonial Gatherer

videoask.com

 MAY

Update Your References Week

First Full Week of May

Get Your Resume in Order

Microsoft Word Resume Assistant

Secret Resume Helper Built into Microsoft Word

nerdybff.com/ resumeassistant

My Perfect Resume

Step-By-Step Resume Creator

myperfectresume.com

Zety

Resume Site with Expert Advice

zety.com

SEPTEMBER

Update Your Resume Month

Even if you're not looking for a job, your resume should be ready to quickly respond to an opportunity. Celebrate Update Your Resume Month in September with **Zety**, an easy resume site with expert advice. Need step-by-step help? **My Perfect Resume** guides you through the process. Or you can just click on **Review > Resume Assistant** in Microsoft Word to access real examples from LinkedIn for your industry and position.

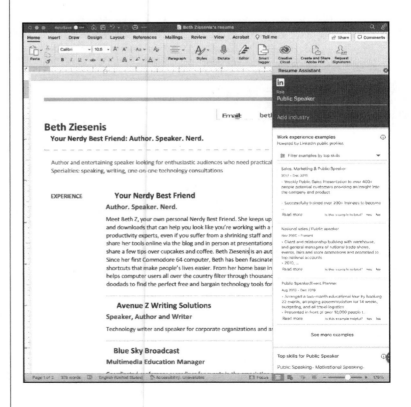

Grow Your Business Knowledge and Career Skill Sets

September is Self-Improvement Month, and it's a great opportunity to grow your business skills and knowledge base. Google has secret free resources with lessons for leadership and more. **Grow with Google** offers free training and tools for small businesses, veterans and other professionals on a number of topics. Some programs, like the certifications, cost money. But Google offers a scholarship program, so don't let that stop you.

Google Primer is a free mobile app with 5-minute lessons for business and marketing. It's a great way to get bite-sized tips to be better at your job. And it's free. We like free.

Google Primer

Free Marketing and Business Lessons on Your Phone

yourprimer.com

Grow with Google

Free and Paid Training and Tools for Career Growth, Business Knowledge and More

grow.google

 SEPTEMBER

Self-Improvement Month

Branding and Naming

Brainstorm New Names for Products, Events and Companies

NamingMagic

Free AI Writing Tool for New Business, Event and Product Name Ideas

namingmagic.com

 FEBRUARY 13

Get a Different Name Day

Get a Different Name Day was meant to be a silly holiday on February 13 to rename yourself for a day. But it's a great opportunity to brainstorm new names for your old products, events and perhaps even a new company. And it's easy enough to do with the AI-powered writing tool called **NamingMagic**.

See If Your Username Is Unique

On National Name Yourself Day (April 9), do some research to see if your username is really yours. Head over to **Namechk** to search for your username to see if it's in use on more than 90 social media sites. You can also check domain names. Namechk also has an extra feature called Name Generator to help you find new names for your business, brand, domain, social media profiles or even Minecraft gamer usernames.

Namechk

Database of Usernames for Social Media Sites and More

namechk.com

 APRIL 9

National Name Yourself Day

Update Your Profile Pic

Whether you are signing up for a new dating app to celebrate National Matchmaker Day on August 31 or not, your profile pic can use an upgrade. **PFPMaker** immediately removes the background from your headshot and frames your image with artsy, modern backgrounds. The color pops are great for standing out on any social platform from LinkedIn and Clubhouse (Page 133) to Hinge and Bumble.

PFPMaker

Tool to Transform Headshots into Stylish Profile Pictures for Social Media

pfpmaker.com

 AUGUST 31

National Matchmaker Day

Vision and Goals

Envision Your Future

VISUAPP

Vision Board and
Goal-Making App

visuapp.github.io

 JANUARY 13

**Make Your Dreams
Come True Day**

 JANUARY

**National Vision
Board Day**

Second Saturday
in January

What does your dream house look like? Your perfect job? Your ultimate vacation? Get creative with the **VISUAPP** to make your vision board on... wait for it... National Vision Board Day, on the second Saturday in January. Curiously enough, Make Your Dreams Come True Day is around the same date (January 13).

Start a Journal

I don't know if you can consider any month the official National Journal Writing Month because its founder celebrates it the first day of January, April, July and October. NaJoWriMo is modeled after National Novel Writing Month (NaNoWriMo), which challenges participants to write 50k words in 30 days.

But journal writing can help you stay focused and articulate your challenges and goals. And if you need help keeping up with your journaling habit, tech has some solutions.

Reflectly is a journaling app that uses artificial intelligence to help you explore your feelings and measure your moods. Its AI features help you analyze trends with mood correlations and graphs, but those features are behind a hefty paywall. But it may be worth it if you're stuck in life and at work. A Harvard Business School study found that workers who spend 15 minutes a day reflecting on their work had a 23 percent higher performance score than the control group*.

Reflectly

AI-Powered Journaling App

reflectly.app

JANUARY, APRIL, JULY & OCTOBER

National Journal Writing Month

First Day of January, April, July and October

*Di Stefano, Giada and Gino, Francesca and Pisano, Gary and Staats, Bradley R., *Making Experience Count: The Role of Reflection in Individual Learning* (June 14, 2016). Harvard Business School NOM Unit Working Paper No. 14-093, Harvard Business School Technology & Operations Mgt. Unit Working Paper No. 14-093, HEC Paris Research Paper No. SPE-2016-1181, Available at: SSRN: **ssrn.com/abstract=2414478** or **http://dx.doi.org/10.2139/ssrn.2414478**

Restructure Your Next Steps

Habitica

Habit-Building App
with Gamification

habitica.com

Way of Life

Super Simple
Habit-Building App

wayoflifeapp.com

 JUNE

**Rebuild Your
Life Month**

New Year's Resolutions are usually reserved for January, but Rebuild Your Life Month in June is another opportunity to focus on building better habits.

Habitica is a game-based habit-building app that rewards you with badges and electronic kudos when you achieve your goals — or throws a little punishment your way when you don't. **Way of Life** is another habit tracker, but this one is super simple and game-free.

Create Something

Image Management

Organize Your Images

ACDSee
Image Organizer and Editor with the Best Name
acdsee.com

Google Photos
Phenomenal Photo/Video Storage with Image Recognition
google.com/photos

iCloud
Apple's Image Storage Solution
icloud.com

Mylio
Image Organizer with Facial Recognition and More
mylio.com

JANUARY

National Clean Up Your Computer Month

FEBRUARY

National Clean Out Your Computer Day

Second Monday in February

The shoebox full of old photos has been replaced by a data-hogging digital folder of images and video clips documenting soccer games, breakfasts and selfies. And both are still just as unorganized as ever. Since January is National Clean Up Your Computer Month, it's time to tackle the 10 jillion megabytes of images you have in 52 file locations.

Don't worry if you don't get this done in January. The second Monday in February is National Clean Out Your Computer Day.

Google Photos and **Apple's iCloud** have made great use of artificial intelligence to help you organize, store and identify your photo memories. They'll also help you create collages, videos and other sharable memory multimedia. You can search by date, location, person and even objects.

ACDSee's name makes me the most nostalgic, but its functionality is top notch. Although it's primarily made for professionals, ACDSee has a plan for individuals that lets you store, manage and edit images and video. It will pull all your images together to help you find duplicates, plus let you batch convert images from one format to another and much more. **Mylio** has similar functionality, and they both use facial recognition and other advanced-search features to help you categorize and sort your images.

Clean Up Your Pictures

Even if you don't celebrate World Photography Day (August 19), you probably have lots of images that need organizing and cleaning up. If you need to add watermarks for branding or borders for aesthetics, you don't have to open them one by one. **PhotoStack** lets you bulk upload, bulk edit and bulk download a bunch of files at once.

Cleanup.pictures is another easy site for removing the empty pizza box from the shot of your board of directors working on the budget. Drag and drop an image into the working area, then use the tool to erase clutter, defects or ex-boyfriends.

On the go, I've never found a background/object remover tool better than **TouchRetouch**. It's easy to use, and it just works! I've edited out power cords, exit signs, coffee cups and much more. It's so helpful when you're trying to clean up pictures to post from your phone.

Cleanup.pictures

Free Site to Remove Unwanted Objects from Images

cleanup.pictures

PhotoStack

Free Bulk Image Editor

photostack.app

TouchRetouch

The Best Mobile Object and Background Remover App

adva-soft.com/ app-pageTouch.html

 AUGUST 19

World Photography Day

Bring Old Photos Back to Life

Bigjpg
Site to Resize Low-Resolution Images without Pixelating
bigjpg.com

bigmp4
Video-Editing Site to Colorize, Enhance and Resize Video Clips
bigmp4.com

jpgHD
Old Photo Restoration Tool
jpghd.com

SEPTEMBER 27

Ancestor Appreciation Day

Whether you're looking to update the online photo album with the old family photos or you're searching through your company's photo archives for a retirement party, you can breathe life into images from the past. On Ancestor Appreciation Day (September 27), check out **jpgHD** for lossless restoration of old photos with AI. When you buy credits ($5 for 50), you can remove tears and folds of the original photo and even animate the faces of your ancestors. It's kinda creepy but way cool.

Sister sites **Bigjpg** and **bigmp4** apply AI to resize low-res pics and colorize and improve videos.

Beth Z, age 7: Before and after jpgHD restoration

Digitize Your Old Photos

I don't know a single person who doesn't have a pile of old family photos hidden in a closet somewhere. Celebrate National Pack Rat Day by unpacking the memories and digitizing them so they're easy to share.

Photomyne lets you snap a picture of multiple photos at once, like photos in a photo album. Then it automatically separates the photos into individual images for fine-tuning and sharing. The company also has other apps such as **FilmBox** to scan negatives using the Photomyne site as a backlight.

Google's **PhotoScan** does the same thing, although I liked the results from Photomyne a little better.

If you have more than a handful of photos to scan, consider a service that does it for you. My sister and I digitized boxes of old photos for my dad with **DigMyPics.** The conversion of his memories is the best present we ever gave him, he says. DigMyPics converts photos for $.39 each. We sent them hundreds of photos through the mail. Within a few days, they were online. We could delete the awful ones and just pay for the ones we wanted to keep. Then they touched them up, organized them and even printed soft-cover thumbnail books as a guide. The money we spent was totally worth it.

CREATE

DigMyPics

Service for Photo Scanning and Video Transfer

digmypics.com

FilmBox

App that Scans Photo Negatives and Converts Them to Digital Images

photomyne.com/filmbox

Photomyne

Photo-Scanning Tools for Old Photos and Negatives

photomyne.com

PhotoScan

Google's Mobile Photo Scanner App

google.com/photos/scan

 MAY 17

National Pack Rat Day

Design Templates

Add a Twist to Your Social Media Graphic Templates

Canva

The World's Best Graphic Template Tool

canva.com

 JUNE

Entrepreneurs "Do It Yourself" Marketing Month

June is Entrepreneurs "Do It Yourself" Marketing Month. Isn't that kind of redundant? Most of us small business folks these days have to do our own marketing, accounting, dishwashing, litter box cleaning…. We're responsible for a lot!

When it comes to graphic templates, **Canva** is the king of the world. Not only does this pioneering site have hundreds of thousands of professionally designed social media graphics… it also has video clips, logo design, t-shirt designs, book covers…. everything. It covers anything you would want to add an image or video to.

The free options on Canva are unbelievable, but for less than the price of a lunch every month, you can upgrade to the pro version for free access to professional graphics and video clips.

Seriously. The pro version is insane. Canva is insane. The options are insane. And you could drive yourself insane playing with everything.

If I had one criticism of Canva, it would be that everyone knows about it. You can see Canva templates on Instagram by the thousands, and it takes some work to create something unique to you and your brand. What's more, most of Canva's competitors have the same types of templates, so there's a lot of wow out there… but it's the same wow as everyone else.

Social Media Graphic Templates (continued)

If you're looking for something beyond Canva, try **Picmaker** (a cousin of Animaker on Page 108), I was impressed. Picmaker has the types of social media templates that everyone does, but they added a feature they call the MAD Button. Pressing the MAD button invokes AI that switches up your colors, graphics, layout, fonts and more. With the MAD Button, you're more likely to end up with a unique-r design. Plus it's fun to push something called the MAD Button.

Picmaker

Graphic Template Tool with AI-Powered Design Ideas

picmaker.com

Instantly Update Your Graphics

Biteable Image Resizer

Site that Instantly Transforms Images into the Right Size for Any Social Media Platform

biteable.com/tools/ image-resizer

Designify

Site that Applies 70+ Layouts to an Image in Seconds

designify.com

Download All Images

Chrome Extension to Download Images from a Site in One Click

download-all-images.mobilefirst.me

PhotoRoom

Mobile App that Applies 70+ Layouts to an Image in Seconds

photoroom.com

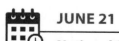 **JUNE 21**

National Selfie Day

Chances are we all have a kabillion photos to post for National Selfie Day on June 21. Try these three instant tools to upgrade your image design and collections.

Designify is so dang cool. Upload one photo, selfie or not, and within about 10 seconds (not exaggerating), Designify generates about 70 social media graphics with different backgrounds, shapes, layouts and more. Then pop over to **Biteable's Image Resizer** to transform one image into the right sizes for every possible social media format... stories to banners to square Insta classics.

Don't have all the selfies on your computer? **Download All Images** will help. It's a Chrome extension that will, ummm, download all the images on a web page. It's a great shortcut for getting all the photos of your board members off the about us page.

One more... if you're on the go, try the mobile app **PhotoRoom** for the same type of image-to-1000 graphics feature.

Design Tools

Let AI Help Your Sketching Skills

Author Diane Alber turned the concept of her book "I'm Not Just a Scribble" into National Scribble Day (March 27) to inspire kids and adults through art.

Google has been training AI to recognize doodles and transform them to clipart. Practice your drawing skills with its challenge called **Quick, Draw!** And then sketch your own masterpieces and let Google replace them with professional icons using **AutoDraw**.

AutoDraw

Google's AI-Powered Doodle Recognition Tool

autodraw.com

Quick, Draw!

Google Pictionary-Type Challenge

quickdraw.withgoogle.com

📅 **MARCH 27**

National Scribble Day

Generate Fake Faces

Generated Photos

Site to Generate AI Faces of
People Who Don't Exist

generated.photos

 MARCH 18

**National Awkward
Moments Day**

Imagine you visit a website to see dozens of smiling fans featured on the front page. It's a diverse group of followers meant to impress visitors. But perhaps if you look closely… I mean REALLY closely, you notice something weird about the people. They are not real people.

The people are all AI-generated faces from the website **Generated Photos**.

Awkward, perhaps even awkward enough to celebrate on March 18, National Awkward Moments Day.

Generated Photos will let you… umm… generate people. Using the latest AI technology, you can generate hundreds of thousands of different faces with different head positions and different skin colors and different ages and different hair lengths and and and….

The images are scarily realistic and represent extensive advances in technology from one of the original AI face sites: thispersondoesnotexist.com. You may not need the stock images on this site, but you should stop by to see how creepy (and addicting) it is to create fake people.

CREATE

GIF Yourself

Celebrate National Humor Month in April by making your own reaction GIFs to add humor to your posts and multimedia all year long.

The site **Unscreen** lets you upload little video clips and remove the background. Film yourself pointing, clapping, dancing and thumbs-up-ing to make transparent GIFs (called stickers) that you can add to images and video. **Removeit.io** does the same and doesn't add a watermark on the free versions.

Removeit.io

Watermark-Free Video Background Remover

removeit.io

Unscreen

Original Site to Remove Video Backgrounds

unscreen.com

 APRIL

National Humor Month

Try Out Some New Color Schemes

Upgrade your color schemes with a color palette generator for National Decorating Month in April. **Coolors** generates color palettes, and you can lock in your key shades and generate more palettes around it. It's fun for hours! You can also tap into the vast Adobe creative empire with the **Adobe Color** tool. Both tools will also analyze colors from an image to make a palette that will make your social media graphics more cohesive.

Adobe Color

Adobe's Color Palette Generator

color.adobe.com

Coolors

Fun and Flexible Color Palette Generator

coolors.co

 APRIL

National Decorating Month

Grab a GIF from Any YouTube Video

Gifs.com
YouTube GIF-Making Site
gifs.com

DECEMBER 3

**National Make
a Gift Day**

Technically December 3 is National Make a Gift Day, but as a nerd, I keep reading it as "Make a *GIF* Day." Create a GIF with any YouTube video by adding the word "gif" before "youtube" in the URL. Add the word "gif" to…

youtube.com/watch?v=hgfxedoV8vA to get… gifyoutube.com/watch?v=hgfxedoV8vA, which will transform to… gifs.com/watch?v=hgfxedoV8vA

The new URL will switch to a site called **Gifs.com** where you can choose a few seconds and make some adjustments.

Note: use the actual YouTube link in your browser bar, not the shortcut link you get from the share button.

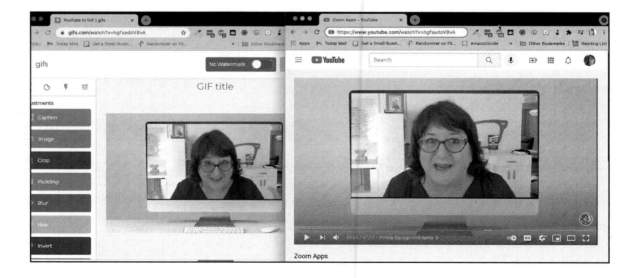

Make Your Own Cartoons

Cartoonists Day is May 5. Celebrate by making your own cartoon with the **Voilà AI Artist Cartoon Photo** app. Or create cartoon characters for explainer videos and presentations with **Pixton**. Another cool cartoonizer tool is **Colorcinch**. Many of their filters are in the pro level, but the variety of effects is impressive. I suppose that's not surprising because Colorcinch used to be Cartoonize, and the website still directs there.

Colorcinch

Cartoonizer and Art Effect Tool

cartoonize.net

Pixton

Cartoon Character Generator

pixton.com

Voilà AI Artist Cartoon Photo

AI-Powered Cartoon Generator for Headshots

linktr.ee/voilaaiartist

MAY 5

Cartoonists Day

CREATE

Discover a New Font

Dafont

Free Font Site with Interactive Preview Feature

dafont.com

Font Squirrel

Free Fonts for Commercial Use

fontsquirrel.com

Google Web Fonts

Font Sets for Online Use

google.com/fonts

 JULY

Comic Sans Day

First Friday of July

The world's most hated font is hands down Comic Sans, which means of course it has its own day. Every first Friday in July, celebrate Comic Sans Day by finding a font other than Comic Sans.

I'm a passionate (obsessed?) font enthusiast, and one of my favorite font-fan sites is **Dafont**.

The key to finding your perfect font on Dafont is to put sample text into the custom preview box and then search by theme (cartoon, curly, calligraphy, handwritten). Most are free for personal use, and many are just plain free. Use filters to find ones you can use commercially. Read the fine print on fonts you use for work because the guidelines for use vary greatly.

Font Squirrel is another great resource, though it doesn't provide a preview of your text. The cool thing about the resources on this site is that they're all free for commercial use, so you won't have the letdown of finding the perfect font and then having to give it up because it's only for personal use.

If you're looking to add a little snazziness to your website, you can find new fonts that will work on the web at **Google Web Fonts**.

Video

Dramatically Speed Up Your Video Editing

If you've ever tried to edit video, you know how long it can take and how easy it is to put it off. September 27 is National No Excuses Day, and it's time to dramatically speed up your video editing chores.

Tools like **Descript** (my favorite) and **Type Studio** transcribe video and audio. Then you can edit the media by just deleting or reorganizing the transcript! Of all the tools in this book, Descript has been the one that has saved me the most time. There's a free version, but the paid is well worth it, especially with the mind-blowing Overdub feature (see Page 104).

Descript

Downloaded Media Editing Tool that Uses Transcripts to Make Edits

descript.com

Type Studio

Online Media Editing Tool that Uses Transcripts

typestudio.co

📅 **SEPTEMBER 27**

National No Excuses Day

Clone Your Voice

Overdub

Voice Clone Feature for the Descript Video Editing Tool

descript.com/overdub

 MARCH 22

International Talk Like William Shatner Day

 MAY 21

Talk Like Yoda Day

March 22 is the day… that we… speak… with… epic… pauses — to celebrate the enigmatic speech patterns of the "Star Trek" star on International Talk Like William Shatner Day.

His voice is almost as distinctive as Yoda's, who has his own day on May 21. Your voice is distinctive, too. And because AI is creepy, you can create a clone of your voice using the **Overdub** tool in Descript (see more info on Descript's video-editing magic on Page 103). You submit recordings of your voice, and Overdub creates a synthetic version that will read out text in your distinctive style. #HelpfulButCreepy

By NBC Television - eBay item photo front photo back, Public Domain, commons.wikimedia.org/w/index.php?curid=20415215

Make a Funny Movie

All of us need to celebrate Let's Laugh Day on March 19, and a fun, exciting video with your favorite pictures and video clips will bring a smile to all watchers.

Magisto takes your photos and short videos and synchronizes them into a multimedia movie complete with a soundtrack. Gather 10 or more pictures and/or videos, throw in a title and choose a theme and soundtrack—then push a button. PRESTO! Magisto instantly creates a perfectly timed, perfectly professional, perfectly awesome video that can showcase your event, your boss's retirement, your kid's prom preparations, your company's products—you name it.

Bonus! Video hosting site **Vimeo** bought Magisto, and now you can get the maker tools in both apps. For about $10 a month through Magisto, you are upgraded to the pro version of Vimeo, which is normally $20 a month.

Magisto
Movie Maker for Video Clips
magisto.com

Vimeo
Video Hosting Site Now with Customizable Video Templates
vimeo.com

 MARCH 19

Let's Laugh Day

CREATE

Illustrate Your Points with Sketchnotes or Whiteboard Videos

Concepts
Sketchnote and Illustration Note App
concepts.app

Doodly
Whiteboard, Blackboard and Glassboard Software
doodly.com

Powtoon
Online Whiteboard and Explainer Video Tool
powtoon.com

VideoScribe
Downloadable Whiteboard Video Tool
videoscribe.co

 JANUARY 11

World Sketchnote Day

Sketchnotes are illustrated notes that pull out the best points and add graphics, color and life. Sketchnote artists are some of the most creative people I've ever met, and of course they have their own day! World Sketchnote Day is January 11, and the **Concepts** app gives you the tools to be your own sketchnote artist.

If you're not an artist at all (that's me), perhaps a whiteboard or explainer video will help you illustrate your points.

Powtoon is a pioneer in low-cost whiteboard generators, which can cost thousands of dollars through a design firm. The online tool lets you start with templates to create presentations and videos. It takes a little finagling to get used to the interface; but when you understand the basics, you can create a brag-worthy showstopper. You can create Powtoon-branded videos and slides for free or buy a subscription starting at $19 a month for an annual plan.

One of my clients made an incredibly impressive whiteboard video using **VideoScribe**, which you can download on your computer or use on an iOS device. The pricing is about the same as Powtoon, and the animations are a little more hand drawn. **Doodly** is another downloadable tool. I like the way it draws in (doodles) chalkboard videos, erasing sections to add more pieces. You can look like a pro with any of the three tools.

Add Captions to Your Videos

Although I can't find the source for this statistic, it's often quoted that 85% of Facebook videos are watched without the audio. National Save Your Hearing Day is May 31, and it's a good time to recognize that your viewing audience may not be listening to your audio because of a preference or an impairment.

I adore today's video tools that automatically transcribe video and audio and animate the text karaoke-style. I use both **Wave.video** and **Milk Video** to create captions on the fly. Both do a great job of transcribing and synching the text with the video. Then I just correct the transcripts, arrange the words in the video template the way I want and publish. It turns a talking-head recording into a dynamic, compelling video.

Wave.video works best for short social media clips. Milk Video is better for excerpts from online programs.

Behind the scenes: I have a soft spot for Milk Video. I was an early adopter, and I've gone back and forth with the team several times about their pricing and the structure. They now have a free version and a super reasonable price for individuals. Yay!

Milk Video

Online Auto-Captioning Video Tool for Video Clips from Meetings

milkvideo.com

Wave.video

Social Media Video Tool with AI-Powered Animated Captions

wave.video

 MAY 31

National Save Your Hearing Day

CREATE

Animate Your Messages

Animaker

Animation Site with Robust
Free Options

animaker.com

Steve.ai

Animation Site for
Text-to-Video AI Creations

steve.ai

 OCTOBER 28

**International
Animation Day**

October 28 is International Animation Day, and these animation video tools will have you obsessed. **Animaker** has a free version that lets you create animated videos from templates.

But wait! There's more. In 2021, Animaker released a tool they call **Steve.ai**. This site lets you write a script for a video, then it uses AI to animate the story you want to tell. As of this writing, the number of template styles are pretty limited. But I was able to write a quick list of my favorite video tools, and I had a passable video in about five minutes (and four of those were the video processing).

Royalty-Free Images, Audio and Video

Discover Interesting, Unusual and Gigantic Royalty-Free Asset Collections

· ·

The first day of the year is Public Domain Day! It's a joyous celebration for lovers of old music, movies and literature. On Public Domain Day, scores of old works lose their copyright and fall into the public domain for royalty-free use.

JANUARY 1

Public Domain Day

Older works are fascinating sources for images, audio and video clips. And on the next few pages you'll find a whole bunch of other options for free and bargain elements you can use without fear of copyright infringement.

Note: Always triple check the rights. It's just good practice.

Gotfryd, B., photographer. (1984) *Steve Jobs Apple computer*. United States, 1984. [Photograph] Retrieved from the Library of Congress, loc.gov/item/2020731396/.]

CREATE

Bigger Collections

Library of Congress

Collection of Images, Books, Audio, Videos and More that the Library of Congress Believes Are Free to Use

loc.gov/free-to-use

New York Public Library Public Domain Collections

Public Domain Downloads with the Coolest Visualization Tools Ever

nypl.org/research/collections/digital-collections/public-domain

Unsplash

Legendary Free Image Site

unsplash.com

Wikimedia Commons

50M+ Free Media Files in a Clunky Search Interface

commons.m.wikimedia.org

Icons

3Dicons

Free 3D Icons in Multiple Formats and Angles

3dicons.co/

Icons8

Insane Number of Customizable Illustrations, Images, Music, 3D Files. Insane.

icons8.com

3Dicons

Icons8

Photos

Canadian Stock Images

Funny (and Free) Stock Images with a Decidedly Canadian Vibe

cira.ca/stock-images

Foodiesfeed

Free Royalty-Free Stock Images of Food

foodiesfeed.com

From Old Books

Free Images from Antique and Vintage Books

fromoldbooks.org

Kaboompics

Beautiful Images with Amazing Search Engine and Color Palette Analyses

kaboompics.com

SplitShire

High-Quality Free Photos and Video

splitshire.com

Canadian Stock Images

Foodiesfeed

SplitShire

Illustrations

3D Bay

Free, Fun 3D Stock Images

clouddevs.com/3dbay/

Blush

Free and Premium Customizable Character Illustrations with Scenes

blush.design

Cleanpng.com

Free Graphics with Transparent Backgrounds

cleanpng.com

Iconduck

More than 100k Free Royalty-Free Icons with a Super Search Engine

iconduck.com

NegativeSpace

Well-Composed, Hi-Res Photos

negativespace.co

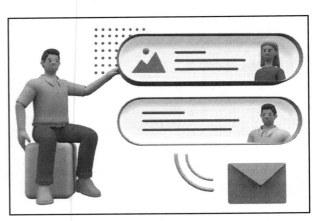

3D Bay

Iconduck

Audio

Free Music Archive
Collection of Free Music by Artists
freemusicarchive.org

Freesound
Free Sound Effects and Audio Clips
freesound.org

Uppbeat
Free and Subscription-Based Audio with Sound Effects and Music
uppbeat.io

YouTube Audio Library
Extensive Collection of Free Royalty-Free Audio and Sound Effects
youtube.com/audiolibrary

Video

Life of Pix
Royalty-Free Images with a Free Video Cousin
lifeofpix.com

Life of Vids
Royalty-Free Videos with a Free Image Cousin
lifeofvids.com

Videvo
Mix of Free and Paid Video Clips and Stock Footage
videvo.net

Put on a Smiley Face

Have you ever noticed the date on the calendar emoji symbol?

Me neither… until I read that July 17 is World Emoji Day. One of the coolest World Emoji Day activities is the highly anticipated World Emoji Awards from **Emojipedia**. This list shares the most popular new emojis and analyzes emoji trends.

Fun fact: The emojis we see everywhere are copyrighted… some by Apple, some by Google and many by JoyPixels. I created my own calendar icon for this book so I didn't have to pay emoji super-designer JoyPixels hundreds of dollars.

You can get royalty-free emojis on sites like **Freepik**, which has millions of royalty-free vectors, images, icons, templates and much more. They are free with attribution and limited daily downloads, or you can subscribe for free rein. **Reshot** also has plenty of icons, vectors and images… and is 100% free with no attribution needed.

Emojipedia
Directory of Emojis with Trends and Variations
emojipedia.org

Freepik
Millions of Vectors, Images, Icons, Themes and Much More
freepikcompany.com

Reshot
100% Free Royalty-Free Icons, Illustrations and Images
reshot.com

 **JULY 17**

World Emoji Day

Spend and Save

Travel

What's Next? Beach or Mountains?

Hopper

Travel Shopping App to Find the Best Time to Fly

hopper.com

Skyscanner

Travel Tool for People with Wanderlust

skyscanner.com

 JANUARY

National Plan for Vacation Day

Last Tuesday of January

 JANUARY

National Shop for Travel Day

Second Tuesday of January

Celebrate National Plan for Vacation Day (last Tuesday of January) by exploring destinations with **Skyscanner**.

When you've decided on your destination, another app comes in handy. The second Tuesday of January is National Shop for Travel Day, so throw some potential dates into the **Hopper** app to discover the best time to buy your tickets. For trips you know are on the horizon, set an alert with Hopper so you get a notification when prices are at their lowest.

Change Your View Without Leaving Home

There's a Virtual Vacation Day (March 30)! What a perfect holiday for what we've been through in the 2020s.

When the pandemic hit in March of 2020, our worlds got a lot smaller. So some clever folks started a site that lets people upload short videos of the views outside their windows to give you a new view of the world. Visit **WindowSwap** online to watch a sunset in San Francisco and twinkling skyscrapers at night from Hong Kong.

WindowSwap

Site for Views from Windows Around the World

window-swap.com

 MARCH 30

National Virtual Vacation Day

SPEND & SAVE

Meet Your Family for Dinner

My brother-in-law travels for work, and sometimes the hubby meets him for a brothers' getaway somewhere in the middle. The discussions usually involve lots of web searching, map reading and brother-to-brother texting.

If only they would ask me about an easier way to find a place to meet, I could save them lots of hassle. **WhatsHalfway.com** helps you find the halfway point for a meetup, perhaps on May 18 for Visit Your Relatives Day.

WhatsHalfway.com

Site to Find Restaurants, Hotels and Other Meetup Places Between Two Points

whatshalfway.com

 MAY 18

Visit Your Relatives Day

Plan a Road Trip

iExit

Interstate Exit Guide

iexitapp.com

Roadtrippers

Road Trip Planner

roadtrippers.com

 MAY

National Road Trip Day

Friday before Memorial Day

AAA warns us every year that Memorial Day weekend is one of the busiest times on the road of the year. That's why it makes sense that the Friday before Memorial Day is National Road Trip Day.

Roadtrippers lets you make your plan to get from A to B, whether you want the most direct route to save money or the drive that brings you past the best hot chicken joints in Nashville. You can use the app or the site to plot start and end points, then have fun with all the possibilities in between. Share your trips with friends to make sure everyone sees what she wants to see.

If the destination is more important for you than the journey on your road trip, you are going to love **iExit**, the app that lists the facilities at every highway exit. Not only will iExit help you find the nearest Wendy's off the highway, it also shows you real-time gas prices to help you fill up without blowing up the budget.

Track Your Mileage Automatically

National Odometer Day (May 12) encourages people to check their odometers and keep up with vehicle maintenance as their vehicles age. The holiday can also remind us that we're losing money by not tracking the mileage we drive for work.

MileIQ is the experienced grandfather of this category, and **Hurdlr** exploded with the growth of DoorDash, Lyft and other gig-economy driving jobs. **Stride** is a 100 percent free option made by a health insurance company. I find that puzzling, but people love it.

Hurdlr

Mileage Tracker for the Gig Economy

Hurdlr.com

MileIQ

Original Automatic Mileage Tracker App

mileiq.com

Stride

Free Mileage Tracker Tool with Expense Management

stridehealth.com/tax

 MAY 12

National Odometer Day

SPEND & SAVE

Shopping

Trust But Verify... Everything

Fakespot

Tool that Reviews the Reviews on Amazon, Walmart and More to Help You Find Fake Ones

fakespot.com

MARCH 29

National Smoke and Mirrors Day

Magicians practice the art of illusion, and National Smoke and Mirrors Day (March 29) celebrates their skills. But in today's world, technology can deceive us very easily. Fight back against fake reviews on Amazon and other shopping sites with **Fakespot**. The tool scans reviews to look for patterns, suspicious reviewers and other red flags we may not be able to see.

The Chrome extension is especially helpful, especially when you're shopping for something like a monitor. You know you want "a big one," but it's hard to tell the differences among the top models.

With the extension, you can sort by the most reliable reviews, and you'll also see highlights from the reviews about the product in one handy list.

Support Black-Owned Businesses

August is National Black Business Month, and **EatOkra** makes it easier. The site offers more than 10k restaurants and food-related businesses owned by people of color. **Miiriya** acts as a marketplace *à la* Etsy for products from black-owned businesses.

EatOkra

Directory of Black-Owned Restaurants and Other Food-Related Businesses

eatokra.com

Miiriya

Marketplace of Products from Black-Owned Businesses

miiriya.com

 AUGUST

National Black Business Month

SPEND & SAVE

Save Money on Prescriptions

October is Organize Your Medical Information Month, but we can use tech to take this idea to the next level.

Use **Medisafe** or **GoodRX** to manage your medications, find the best prices and discover coupons. GoodRX alone has saved me more than $500 over the years, and it's free. We love free.

GoodRX

Prescription Bargain Finder and Medication Manager

goodrx.com

Medisafe

Medication Monitor and Reminder with Coupon Tools

medisafeapp.com

 OCTOBER

Organize Your Medical Information Month

Find the Best Airfare

TripIt

Travel Organizer with
Price-Watching Pro Version

tripit.com

 AUGUST 23

Cheap Flight Day

I've never heard of Cheap Flight Day (August 23), but with the Pro version of **TripIt**, I feel like I don't have to depend on one day to find the best price.

TripIt organizes all the details for my flights and puts them into handy cards on the app. The free version is handy, but TripIt Pro is totally worth it. For about $50 a year, TripIt monitors my booked flights and notifies me when the price drops. Over the years I've gotten back way more than I have paid for the subscription.

Budgets

Set Up a Budget

Almost half of Americans aren't saving enough for retirement. Perhaps it's because they don't have a good budget tool.

Mint is one of the best, year after year. Another award-winning option is **You Need a Budget**. And if you're budgeting with a partner, try **Honeydue**.

Honeydue

Finance Manager for Couples

honeydue.com

Mint

Award-Winning Budget Management Tool

mint.com

You Need a Budget

Four-Rule Budget Management Tool

youneedabudget.com

 OCTOBER

National Retirement Security Week

Third Week in October

SPEND & SAVE

Share Expenses with Friends

Splitwise

Bill-Splitting Tool for
Sharing Expenses

splitwise.com

OCTOBER 17

**National Pay Back
a Friend Day**

Avoid the awkward discussions on National Pay Back a Friend Day (October 17) by figuring out how much everyone owes before the bill comes at dinner. **Splitwise** helps groups divide expenses and chip in for trips, gifts and more.

Find a New Accounting Tool

Wave

Free Accounting System

waveapps.com

NOVEMBER 10

**International
Accounting Day**

As a small business owner, **Wave** is my favorite free tool. I can't believe how many people don't know about it.

It's a super easy online accounting system with invoicing, budgeting, expense tracking and more. It even works for personal budgeting. Give Wave a try on November 10 to celebrate International Accounting Day.

Squirrel Away Money Without Knowing It

Many of us remember the day we walked into a bank and opened our first checking account. The fact that National Online Bank Day (the second Monday in October) exists means that ritual may have gone the way of the fax machine.

Since October 12 is National Savings Day, modernize the way you save money for retirement or a rainy day with apps like **Acorns** and **Digit**. They round up your purchases or sneak small amounts away to help you save and invest.

Acorns

Tool that Invests Your Spare Change Roundups

acorns.com

Digit

AI-Based Savings Tool that Sneaks Small Withdrawals Based on Cash Flow

digit.co

 OCTOBER

National Online Bank Day

Second Monday in October

 OCTOBER 12

National Savings Day

SPEND & SAVE

Keep Track of Your Subscriptions

Truebill

Subscription Monitoring and
Bill Management

truebill.com

 MAY 4

**National
Renewal Day**

National Renewal Day every May 4 is technically a celebration of looking at life anew. But it's better to use it as an opportunity to check the subscriptions in your world that are on auto-renew.

Truebill will keep track of your subscriptions and alert you that you're paying for things you may not be using (#mygymmemberships).

Learn and Grow

LEARN AND GROW

Learning and Homework

Spend the Day Learning

Mental Floss

Smart Stories, Trivia and Fun Facts

mentalfloss.com

TED SMRZR

Site that Transcribes and Summarizes TED Talks

tedsmrzr.vercel.app

TED Talks

Short, Fascinating Videos on Almost Every Topic Imaginable

ted.com

 OCTOBER 22

Smart Is Cool Day

October 22 is Smart Is Cool Day, so don't feel guilty about binging **TED Talks** videos today. What? No time to watch? Use the **TED SMRZR** to read the transcription or browse an AI-powered summary. It also lets you compare the key points of two TED Talks on similar topics.

You can't beat **Mental Floss** for fascinating facts, entertaining education and practical posts. The Mental Floss magazine is no longer in print, and nerd super show "The Big Bang Theory" finale was in 2019. But you can see Mental Floss magazines on Sheldon and Leonard's coffee table in reruns.

Absorb Knowledge Five Minutes at a Time

When we think about a holiday called Chaos Never Dies Day (November 9), what may come to mind is the chaos in your professional world that keeps you from keeping up with information that will keep you updated in your profession and career.

Check out **Uptime**, a summary site that packages lessons into five-minute bits of books, courses and documentaries you need to see.

Uptime

Award-Winning App with Five-Minute "Knowledge Hacks" from Books, Courses, Documentaries and More

uptime.app

 NOVEMBER 9

Chaos Never Dies Day

Solve a Math Problem Without Doing Math

Google Lens Homework Mode

AI-Powered Problem-Solving with the Google Lens Feature

lens.google

Microsoft Math Solver

Microsoft's Visual Math Problem Solver

math.microsoft.com

Pi Day

Pi Day Site with Resources, Education and Math Help

piday.org

 MARCH 14

Einstein's Birthday

International Day of Mathematics

Pi Day

Pi Day is celebrated on March 14… 3.14. People loved the math theme so much that it's also the International Day of Mathematics. Bonus: it's also Albert Einstein's birthday. The nerd power is strong.

If you'd rather celebrate Pi Day with actual pie than doing math problems, check out the problem-solving AI in **Google Lens Homework Mode** and **Microsoft Math Solver**. You just scroll your phone's camera over a math problem (typed or handwritten), and the solution appears on the screen. See? You really didn't have to learn how to solve a quadratic formula.

Calculate and Research Weird but Helpful Stuff

May 11 is National Eat What You Want Day, and if what you want is donuts, **Omni Calculator's** Do or Donut Calculator that tells you how many hours of cuddling you will need to burn off a donut.

Donuts not your thing? Try the Taco Bar Calculator to see how much salsa you need to buy for a party of six, or the Lost Socks Calculator to find out the probability that you'll end up with sock orphans in your laundry.

Omni Calculator also has serious tools like conversions and camera speeds. But it'll also let you know how many **Wolfram | Alpha** helium balloons you'll need to fly.

What? You've never heard of Wolfram | Alpha? It's the craziest info site I've ever seen. How many Scrabble points is the word "nerd," or what's your relationship to your uncle's uncle's son's daughter's cousin or ANYTHING ELSE that can be looked up, calculated, analyzed or configured??!! Wolfram | Alpha has the answers.

Omni Calculator

Site with Hundreds of Silly and Serious Calculators

omnicalculator.com

Wolfram|Alpha

Insight to All the World's Knowledge (More or Less)

wolframalpha.com

 MAY 11

National Eat What You Want Day

Language and Listening

Grow Your Foreign Language Vocabulary While You Surf

Drops

Language Learning in Bite-Sized Pieces with Games and Mnemonics

languagedrops.com

Duolingo

The O.G. Free Language-Learning Tool

duolingo.com

Memrise

Award-winning Language-Learning Tool with Focus on Real-World Interactions

memrise.com

Toucan

Chrome Extension that Helps You Learn a New Language While You Surf

jointoucan.com

 DECEMBER

National Learn a Foreign Language Month

December is National Learn a Foreign Language Month! Although there are plenty of apps and resources where you can go to study a new language, it's easy to forget to make the effort to open them. The **Toucan** extension hangs out with you while you surf and randomly translates words on the page to the language you want to learn.

Well, the process is not quite random because Toucan knows your language level and chooses words and phrases that help you level up without having to make a conscious effort to start a lesson. It's free for the basic level or about five bucks a month for more language training and games. And the little toucan mascot is adorable.

You'll find plenty of interesting language tools around, but three more of my favorites are **Drops**, **Duolingo** and **Memrise**.

Text Like a Digital Native

The goal of Intergeneration Month in September is to bring different generations together. Start with learning the lingo of Generation Z with emoji translator tools like **EmojiTranslate**. In addition to emoji translations, another tool called **LingoJam** will translate Jar Jar Binks, Morse Code and even let you create your own.

EmojiTranslate

Site that Generates Emoji-Filled Text

emojitranslate.com

LingoJam

Comical (and Strange) Translation Site for Emoji and More

lingojam.com

 SEPTEMBER

Intergeneration Month

Listen and Learn on an Audio-Only Social Platform

Although the goal of New Conversations Day on July 12 is to help people ask real questions and start deeper conversations, a hip way to celebrate is to give an audio-only social media platform a try. **Clubhouse** launched in the middle of the pandemic and grew a huge following. Facebook and LinkedIn and even Spotify created rivals because Clubhouse is so popular.

Clubhouse

Audio-Only Social Media Platform for Conversations and Listening

clubhouse.com

 JULY 12

New Conversations Day

Research

Check Facts and Find Resources

Journalist Studio

Site for Fact Checking
and Research

journaliststudio.google.com

NOVEMBER 4

**Use Your Common
Sense Day**

November 4 is Use Your Common Sense Day, but it takes more than common sense to separate fact from fiction online these days.

I have a master's degree in journalism, but my days as a reporter were in a different world. These days journalists have the knowledge of the universe at their fingertips, but their job is much, much harder than mine ever was. Journalists have to sort through massive amounts of misinformation, international censorship and secrecy, plus the fight to get the attention of their audiences, who are bombarded with ads, sites and social media platforms all fighting for their online eyes.

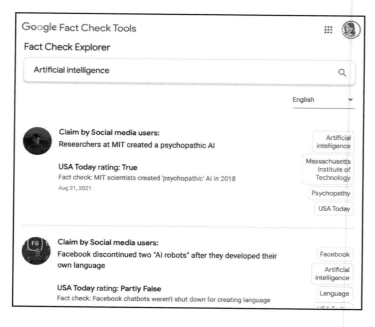

Google created **Journalist Studio** with a host of features that make their jobs just a little bit easier. The studio includes tools from advanced research tools to fact-checking search engines to fancy, showy data visualization tools. Plus Google offers advanced privacy and security services so journalists have a layer of protection from people and governments that seek to undermine investigations.

Seek Out Balanced Articles Online

Tell the Truth Day is July 7, but truth is hard to define in our divided world. We've all struggled with misinformation on the web and trying to verify if something we read is true.

A site called **The Factual** analyzes stories on the web and assigns them a score based on diversity of sources, factual tone of writing, author's expertise and more. You can use the Chrome Plugin or their companion site, **IsThisCredible**, to check articles you come across, and their apps and newsletter offer balanced stories on trending topics.

IsThisCredible

AI-Vetted News Articles and Fact Check Site

isthiscredible.com

The Factual

Algorithm-Based Grading Platform Service that Grades the Factuality of Online Articles

thefactual.com

 JULY 7

Tell the Truth Day

Check Out Older Versions of Web Pages

Wayback Machine

Archive of Snapshots
of Web Pages from the
Internet Archive

web.archive.org

 DECEMBER 8

**Pretend To Be a
Time Traveler Day**

Grab a flapper dress, don a headband and stroll around telling people you were just sipping a gin cocktail in a New York City speakeasy when a phonebooth appeared that transported you to the 21st Century. Yep, that's what Pretend to Be a Time Traveler Day is all about.

The **Wayback Machine** is the internet's version of time travel. Another feature of the awesome Internet Archive is the web's version of time travel. The Wayback Machine captures copies of websites and preserves them so you can see what sites looked like back in the day. This is a great tool for seeking out information that disappeared from a site (remember… nothing ever disappears from the internet). It's also a great way to get perspective on past designs and the evolution of a site.

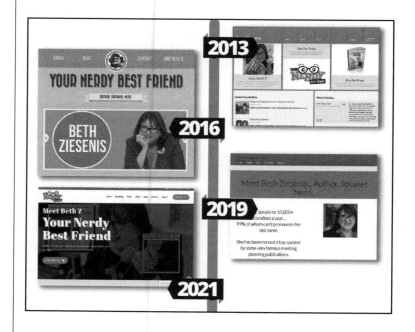

Expand Your World

Arts and Culture

Take a Cultural Trip Around the World

Google Arts & Culture

Tool for Virtual Tours, Digital Art and Online Culture

artsandculture.google.com/ project/street-view

APRIL 18
World Heritage Day

MAY 18
International Museum Day

April 18 is World Heritage Day and the International Day for Monuments and Sites. One month later is International Museum Day.

It's insanely easy to get lost in all the arts and culture on Google's cool site called **Google Arts & Culture**. Tour museums, visit landmarks, view mosaics of famous artworks by color and play crossword puzzles with art and photos. It's easy to spend an hour or more on the site then switch to the mobile apps for more interactive art fun.

Explore the Ocean Depths (and Waste Some Time)

I don't know who Neal is, but his site, **Neal.fun** is awesome. He has a dozen or so pages that you can't help but explore. Put in your birthdate to see the ages of notable figures on Who Was Alive?, then watch the Baby Map to see countries flash every time a new life enters the world. For World Ocean Day (June 8), get a scientific perspective with The Deep Sea and The Size of Space. So much fun stuff.

Neal.fun

Collection of Strange/ Fun/WTH Sites for an Afternoon of Fun and Learning

neal.fun

 JUNE 8

World Ocean Day

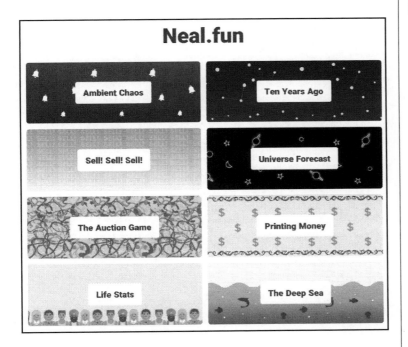

Neal.fun

- Ambient Chaos
- Ten Years Ago
- Sell! Sell! Sell!
- Universe Forecast
- The Auction Game
- Printing Money
- Life Stats
- The Deep Sea

EXPAND WORLD

Enjoy Unusual Art

AmperArt

Works of Art Created
from Ampersands

amperart.com

📅 **SEPTEMBER 8**

**National
Ampersand Day**

I kind of don't know what to say about a website dedicated to art made with ampersand… except you just gotta see it. No wonder the artist founded National Ampersand Day (September 8). Take a break today and just enjoy the quirkiness and creativity on **AmperArt**.

Discover an Old Map

**David Rumsey
Map Collection**

Old Map Resource with
Interactive Overlays

davidrumsey.com

Old Maps Online

Resource for Old Maps

oldmapsonline.org

📅 **APRIL 5**

**Read a
Road Map Day**

When was the last time you tried to refold a road map and stuff it in your glove box? April 5 is National Read a Road Map Day. The site **Old Maps Online** aggregates thousands of (believe it or not) old maps and lets you search geographically and by time period. And the **David Rumsey Map Collection** site (one of the major contributors to Old Maps Online) lets you overlay an old map over present day.

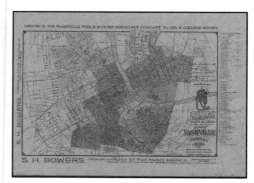

Travel Into the Past with Old Newspapers

Another high-tech holiday is April 7th's International Snail-papers Day for printed newspapers. Like Road Map Day, the online resources for the archives are fascinating (and time sucking).

This article talks about my ancestor Harry Ziesenis, who at the age of 18 built a wireless telegraph plant. I consider this the proof of a hereditary nerd gene in the Ziesenis family. I found the newspaper in a treasure trove of historic American newspapers from a Library of Congress initiative called **Chronicling America**.

Chronicling America

Treasure Trove of Old Newspapers

chroniclingamerica.loc.gov

APRIL 7

International Snailpapers Day

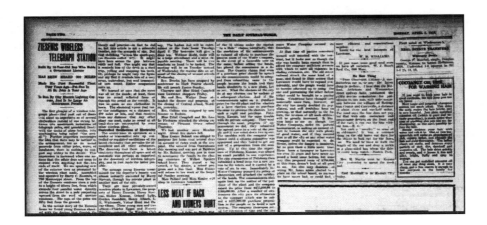

Books and Reading

Pick Out a Great Book Then Tidy Up Your Bookcase

Whichbook

Book Discovery Site Based on Story Characteristics

whichbook.net

 JANUARY

Library Shelfie Day

Fourth Wednesday
in January

How do you arrange books in your bookshelf? Snap a picture and post a "Shelfie" on Library Shelfie Day, the fourth Wednesday in January.

Is your "Shelfie" looking a little bare? Go find your next book on **Whichbook**, where you can find book suggestions based on characteristics such as mood and emotion. You can use sliders to choose between extremes such as "safe vs. disturbing," "optimistic vs. bleak," "expected vs. unpredictable" and even "beautiful vs. disgusting."

Enjoy Your Local Library

National Reading Day is January 23. Check your new book out for free with the public library lending app **Libby** or watch the movie version with another library lending app, **Hoopla**.

Hoopla

Public Library Lending App for Videos, Music, Audiobooks, Comics and Ebooks

hoopladigital.com

Libby

Public Library Lending App for Ebooks and Audiobooks

libbyapp.com

 JANUARY 23

National Reading Day

Pick Up a Good (E)Book

About three years before Amazon released the Kindle E-Reader, author Rita Toews was a little frustrated that ebooks were slow to catch on. So she registered "Read an Ebook Week" for the first full week of March.

Authors and publishers still celebrate, offering thousands of ebooks for great discounts or even free. Indie ebook publisher **Smashwords** organizes the event and maintains a database of more than 80,000 titles you can download for free.

Smashwords

Indie Ebook Publisher Site with Thousands of Free Ebooks

smashwords.com

 MARCH

Read an Ebook Week

First Full Week of March

Listen to a Great Book

Audible

Audiobook Service
from Amazon

audible.com

Internet Archive

Free Audiobooks, Movies
and Much, Much More

archive.org

LibriVox

Audio Recordings of Books
in the Public Domain

librivox.org

 JUNE

**Audiobook
Appreciation Month**

June is Audiobook Appreciation Month, and as an **Audible** addict, I can testify that recorded books have come a long way from your grandpa's books on tape service. I find Audible to be totally worth the membership price (starting at $7.95/month). And you can get plenty of free audiobooks from the audio collections on the **Internet Archive**, including the audiobook collection from **LibriVox**.

Grab a Free Comic Book

It's a Nerd Fest! The first Saturday in May, comic book stores and comics publishers team up to offer free comics to encourage a love of the format and to promote small businesses. The **Free Comic Book Day** website helps you find participating stores and comic books.

Free Comic Book Day

Event Page for Comic Book Stores Giving Away Freebies

freecomicbookday.com

MAY

Free Comic Book Day

First Saturday in May

EXPAND WORLD

Nature and Outdoors

Look for the Rainbows

RainbowFinder

App to Predict Where and
When Rainbows Will Appear

rainbowfinderapp.com

 APRIL 3

**National Find a
Rainbow Day**

Why are there so many songs about rainbows but so few apps? **RainbowFinder** could be the only tech tool that identifies the weather and atmospheric conditions that produce a rainbow. It's the perfect app to download for National Find a Rainbow Day on April 3.

Say Thanks to Your Aloe Vera

Planta

Houseplant ID and Care App

getplanta.com

 JANUARY 10

**Houseplant
Appreciation Day**

The Gardener's Network created Houseplant Appreciation Day to encourage people to adopt and care for a green roommate or two. They chose January 10 because they figure that you were too busy over the holidays to give your plants the attention they deserve.

Download **Planta** to care for your houseplants in classic nerdy style. The app will help ID your plants and guide you to the best care. You can also set reminders and use the light meter to find the best spot.

Enjoy the Great Outdoors

Not only is June the Great Outdoors Month and National Pollinator Month, the first Saturday in June is also National Trails Day. It's like all the holidays are conspiring to get you outside.

Figure out where you're going with the **AllTrails** trail map app. Then figure out what plants, animals and bugs you discover along the way with **Seek by iNaturalist**. And you can join a community of people observing nature and wildlife with the **iNaturalist** app.

AllTrails

Trail Maps for Hiking, Biking and Off-Roading

alltrails.com

iNaturalist

Identification App for Plants and Animals with Community Connections and Observation Reporting

iNaturalist.org

Seek by iNaturalist

App to Identify Creepies, Crawlies and Green Things

inaturalist.org/pages/ seek_app

 JUNE

National Trails Day

First Saturday of June

 JUNE

Great Outdoors Month

National Pollinator Month

Gaze Upon the Stars

SkyView

Augmented Reality
Stargazing App

terminaleleven.com

APRIL 14

**Look Up
at the Sky Day**

Gazing at the sky on a clear night is a pleasure you should share with people you love, and Look Up at the Sky Day (April 14) is the perfect opportunity to start.

Download the **SkyView** app to use its augmented reality features to bring the sky to life. It will superimpose constellations, stars, planets and other heavenly bodies onto the dark sky so you can finally find Orion's Belt. The app also keeps up with sightings and events such as meteor showers and satellite flybys.

Visit a National Park

**National Park Service
App (NPS Mobile)**

Interactive Tool for Visits
to National Parks

nps.gov

NOVEMBER 17

**National Take
a Hike Day**

Take National Take a Hike Day (November 17) to a whole new level with **NPS Mobile**, the revamped version of the National Park Service's app. Every national site is included, including monuments, historic sites, battlefields and parks. The app includes interactive maps, audio tours, extra tips and tools to keep track of and share your travels. In addition to the mobile tool, check the NPS site for plenty of park insights.

Manage and Maintain

MANAGE

DIY and Maintenance

Upgrade Your DIY Skills

DoItYourself

Site with Home Repair and Improvement Help

doityourself.com

iFixit

Lessons and Tips to Repair and Improve Household and Office Items

ifixit.com

 MARCH 11

National Worship of Tools Day

When I moved to Tuscaloosa to start grad school at The University of Alabama, my father gifted me a plastic tub filled with tools that I would need to fix things on my own. I love the hammers, screwdrivers and other tools that Papa picked out for me.

That's why National Worship of Tools Day makes sense. On March 11, we should head to the garage (or the plastic bin) to clean, reorganize and perhaps use the tools of home repair. If you're like me, you have an assortment of tools and a whole list of home repairs you can use them on... but you don't have the knowledge.

Yes, YouTube has thousands (millions?) of how-to videos, but the site **iFixit** is dedicated to these kinds of lessons. The site has advice for everything from getting your &*@%! printer to hook up with your computer to repairing the arm on Mr. Potato Head.

DoItYourself is another free site with both repair and home improvement projects.

Use an App to Measure Spaces and Objects

Celebrate Take a Wild Guess Day on April 15 by guessing how many jellybeans are in a jar at a carnival, or by calculating whether a big-screen TV will fit in the back of a Prius*. Both Apple and Google created measuring tools, both named **Measure**. But Google killed its Measure off in 2021 because that's what Google does sometimes.

Augmented reality apps first ask you to scan the floor so the sensors can get the perspective and understand where your phone is in a 3D world. You can point the viewfinder around the room to place virtual markers on surfaces, walls or floors. As you pan to the end of your measuring area, a virtual line follows you, measuring out the distance.

I have never found these things to be very accurate. I always have trouble anchoring the points where they need to be, and I never trust the findings and end up going to find the tape measure anyway. But they give you a pretty good estimate, and the Apple app is free.

My real estate friends love **magicplan** to measure room sizes and create floor plans. Instead of having to spend an hour walking from room to room with a tape measure, they scan each area to mark the corners and room features. Use magicplan to estimate your square footage or how much paint and trim you need to renovate.

magicplan
Measuring App for Floor Plans
magicplan.app

Measure (Apple)
Apple's Augmented Reality Measuring App
In the App Store

 APRIL 15

Take a Wild Guess Day

*No, a big-screen TV does not fit in the back of a Prius. In fact, the attempt at a purchase at Wal-Mart caused so much giggling by staff members that they actually took a photo of the box sticking awkwardly out of my hatchback so they could show their friends.

Find the Part Replacement for Your Fridge Light Bulb

ManualsLib

Online Database of Product Manuals

manualslib.com

 JANUARY 14

Organize Your Home Day

If you're like me and you can't open your junk drawer anymore because you've stuffed appliance manuals in there, it's time to celebrate Organize Your Home Day on January 14. Ditch all the paper manuals and head over to **ManualsLib**, a free database with manuals for more than 100k brands.

Get Out Those Stubborn Stains

American Cleaning Institute Cleaning Tips

Site with Comprehensive List of Cleaning Tips for Stains, Surfaces and Much More

cleaninginstitute.org/ cleaning-tips

 FEBRUARY 11

Don't Cry Over Spilled Milk Day

To celebrate Don't Cry Over Spilled Milk Day on February 11, you should focus on letting go of things you have no control over.

But if you've actually spilled milk, you may have bigger problems. Bookmark the **American Cleaning Institute's** site to search for solutions to every possible stain, spill and smudge problem you might encounter.

Throw Out the Old Mayo

To prepare for the holiday eating season, plan to celebrate National Clean Out Your Refrigerator Day November 15. You can use the USDA's tool **FoodKeeper** (online and via apps) to store food items properly and avoid food waste.

FoodKeeper

USDA's Food Safety and Storage Tool

nerdybff.com/foodkeeper

 NOVEMBER 15

National Clean Out Your Refrigerator Day

Accessorize Your Yoga Pants

I bet the woman who declared the first Friday in February Working Naked Day had no idea 2020 was coming. I'm all for yoga pants and fuzzy slippers, but please, don't celebrate this holiday.

Instead try **Acloset** or **Cladwell** to catalog your clothing items, get everything organized and discover new ways to wear the same old yoga pants.

Acloset

AI-Driven Clothes Organizer with Weather-Based Style Recommendations

acloset.app

Cladwell

Style Guide and Clothes Organizer App

cladwell.com

 FEBRUARY

Working Naked Day

First Friday in February

MANAGE

Family Management

Keep an Eye on Your Family

Google Family Link
Free Parental Control Tool from Google
families.google.com/familylink

Life360
Family Tracking App
life360.com

 DECEMBER 15
National Cat Herders Day

Every time you try to plot your family members' whereabouts, you're celebrating National Cat Herders Day, whether it's December 15 or not.

Google Family Link is a free parental control tool for devices, content and finding family members. **Life360** has the same types of features. I prefer not to call them "stalking" tools… but that's what they are.

Bring Your Family Together

MyEvent
Family Reunion (and More) Event Manager
myevent.com

 JULY
National Family Reunion Month

One of the toughest challenges of the pandemic was the isolation. Families and groups miss each other, which has caused a spike in personal travel.

Celebrate National Family Reunion Month in July by using **MyEvent** to create a website, collect registration fees, set up a family tree and organize activities.

Help Your Caregivers Stay Organized

If you provide care for a loved one, you have my respect. Providing care and support to others while you juggle your own life's tasks is one of the most generous and toughest jobs you'll ever have.

The third Friday in February is National Caregivers Day. Caregivers can get support from their communities and coordinate the tasks, errands, updates and calendars of the people they care for by creating caregiving circles with **Caring Village** and **CircleOf**. And when neighbors reach out to ask, "What can I do to help?", you can coordinate meals and more with **Lotsa Helping Hands**.

Caring Village

Caregiving Platform with Product Recommendations and Checklists

caringvillage.com

CircleOf

Free App for Unpaid Caregivers

circleof.com

Lotsa Helping Hands

Community Organizing Tool for Meals and Help

lotsahelpinghands.com

FEBRUARY

National Caregivers Day

Third Friday in February

MANAGE

Get Help for Military Families

Hero Care

Red Cross Resource App for the Military Community

Text "GETHEROCARE" to 90999

 NOVEMBER 11

Veterans Day

My husband is a veteran, and November 11, Veterans Day, is one he holds sacred. People in the military and their families can struggle to get the help they need for the unique circumstances that surround the challenges of military service.

The American Red Cross' **Hero Care** app lets families set up and submit an emergency request no matter where in the world service members are stationed. The app also highlights other Red Cross military assistance services, plus offers links to VA facility locations, benefits, mental health resources and career info.

Stay Healthy

STAY HEALTHY

Health

Diagnose that Sniffle

Ada
AI-Powered Medical
Advisor App
ada.com

AskMD
Medical Care and Follow Up
sharecare.com/static/askmd

 FEBRUARY

National Sickie Day

First Monday
of February

In the U.K., the first Monday of February is the day more workers call in sick.

You could Google what could be causing your hacking cough. Wouldn't it be nice if someone followed up in a few days to see if you're doing better? **AskMD** from Sharecare does just that.

Ada is powered by artificial intelligence, the result of many, many data points about your symptoms and the possible outcomes. I like that both will encourage you to check back in so the system can keep monitoring your improvement.

Both AskMD and Ada guide you through a series of questions to narrow down the choices. Then they both lead to guidance toward treatment, whether it is something you can do yourself or if you need to seek advice from medical professionals.

Capture All the Details from a Doctor's Visit

The second Tuesday in June is Call Your Doctor Day, but sometimes conversations about our health are hard to comprehend and harder to get all the details from.

I so wish I had a tool like **Abridge** during my mother's eight-year battle with cancer. Take the app to your medical appointments. It records the conversation and uses AI to extract and define the medical jargon, diagnoses and medication. It will track your health and help you keep up with important information without having to take notes and listen at the same time.

Abridge

Recording Tool for Medical Visits to Decipher Treatments, Medications and Diagnoses

abridge.com

 JUNE

Call Your Doctor Day

Second Tuesday in June

Help Your Nerdy Friends Step Away from the Computer

Some of us nerdy types don't get much sun because we're glued to our hobbies indoors. National Hike with a Geek Day on June 20 encourages people to grab their nerdy friends by the elbow and force them into the sunshine.

If your geeky friend has allergies like mine, look up the day's pollen count with the allergy app **klarify** before you leave the house. Achoo!

klarify

Allergy Tracker with Real-Time Pollen Updates

klarify.me

 JUNE 20

National Hike with a Geek Day

Check Your Skin

Miiskin

Mole-Tracking App

miiskin.com

SkinVision

Skin Check Tool with AI Analysis for Risk Level Assessment

skinvision.com

 JUNE

Beautiful in Your Skin Month

June is Beautiful in Your Skin Month. Not only is it a reminder for us to feel confident about our features and forgive our flaws… it's also a great opportunity to check your skin for potential problems.

Miiskin and **SkinVision** are apps that help you track moles and skin abnormalities while we work with dermatologists to keep our skin healthy.

Burn Calories at Your Desk

Hypocrite alert!

As I write about National Move More Month (April), I realize I've been sitting in this chair for 5.3 hours straight. Don't be like me. Give these fitness tools a try.

Wakeout was the Apple App of the Year in 2020. I vowed to limit the tools in this book to ones that you can find on at least two platforms (Apple, Android, PC, web, etc.). But I feel obliged to include Wakeout because I bought it specifically for the marathon writing sessions for this book. Plus, the site gives you a bunch of samples, so perhaps that counts as web-based access?

Wakeout is designed to help you get little bursts of movement in your home office, and I love it. From the kitchen-based "Fridge Scan Squats" to the seated "Coffee Worship" arm bends, the little exercises will make you move and smile.

If you're not an Apple fan, **MyFitnessPal** has millions of loyal followers for activity and calorie tracking.

MyFitnessPal
Powerful Fitness and Nutrition Tool
myfitnesspal.com

Wakeout
Short Movement Exercise App Designed for Desk Workers (iOS)
wakeout.app

 APRIL

National Move More Month

Emergency and First Aid

Brush Up on Your First Aid Skills

Red Cross First Aid App

App for Training and Advice for First Aid

Text "GETFIRST" to 90999

Red Cross First Aid Smart Speaker Tool

Smart Speaker First Aid Advice and Training

Enable on Alexa or Google Assistant

 SEPTEMBER

World First Aid Day

Second Saturday in September

World First Aid Day is the second Saturday in September to raise awareness of how first aid can save lives and to encourage people to learn first aid skills. Start your first aid studies by downloading the **Red Cross First Aid** app, then enable the skill on your smart speakers.

Prepare for Emergencies

I moved from earthquake country in San Diego into tornado territory in Tennessee. We keep flashlights, emergency supplies, shelf-stable foods and other emergency essentials at hand. These are some of the steps that the U.S. government's site **Ready** recommends. Every September the campaign urges people to prep during National Preparedness Month.

Check out the site for resources to make your plan for everything from helping people with disabilities to mapping evacuation routes. They recommend the **FEMA App** for emergency alerts, safety tips, shelter resources and planning.

Another tech tip: find the precise location of every 3 x 3-meter square in the world with **what3words**. Every square is identified by three words, which means if you followed directions to dudes.celebration.retract, you'd end up at Charlie Daniels Park, the best place in my town to play Pokémon Go. This not only helps you find friends at a festival… it also can help emergency services find you or let you locate a location after a natural disaster when all the landmarks are gone.

FEMA App

FEMA's Mobile Resources for Emergency Preparedness and Help

fema.gov

Ready

U.S. Government Site for Disaster Preparedness and Resources

ready.gov

what3words

Precise Location System for Every 3-Meter Square in the World

what3words.com

 SEPTEMBER

National Preparedness Month

STAY HEALTHY

Self-Care and Mental Health

Retreat and Recover

SoundPrint

Sound-Level Measuring App that Helps You Find Quiet Places to Work

soundprint.co

JANUARY 2

World Introvert Day

After New Year's Day, we introverts need a nap. That is why you'll find us in a corner somewhere quietly celebrating World Introvert Day on January 2.

Find a quiet place to recover with **SoundPrint**, an app that measures noise levels in public places and recommends quiet spots. Apple Watch owners also have a noise level monitor built in.

Take a Deep Breath

Breathe from Calm

Site for Deep Breathing Exercises

calm.com/breathe

eXHALeR

Customizable Breathing Exercises Online

xhalr.com

APRIL

Stress Awareness Month

Stress Awareness Month comes every April to bring attention to the effects of stress and ways to find relief.

The meditation tool Calm created a simple page called **Breathe** that guides you through a few calming deep breaths. If you want to customize your breath exercise, check out **eXHALeR**.

Get a Good Night's Sleep

January 3 is the Festival of Sleep Day. I have some bad news for those of us who like sleep apps, though. Studies have found that few apps that claim to help you monitor your sleep are tested scientifically. And the ones that have show weak correlation to standard sleep tests.

Instead of a sleep app, try mediation podcasts/services like **10 Percent Happier**, **Calm**, **Headspace** and **Insight Timer** to help you disconnect from the world and get better sleep. I'm a huge fan of **Sleep Meditations for Women**.

10 Percent Happier
Positive Podcast for Help with Self Care
tenpercent.com

Calm
Mediation and Sleep Tools
calm.com

Headspace
Another Meditation and Sleep Tool
headspace.com

Insight Timer
Meditation and Sleep Platform with Free Options
insighttimer.com

Sleep Meditations for Women
Free Meditations and Sleep Help Focused on a Female Audience
womensmeditationnetwork.com

 JANUARY 3

Festival of Sleep Day

Take a Power Nap

Pzizz

Sleep Management App

pzizz.com

MARCH

**National
Napping Day**

The First Monday after
Daylight Savings

MARCH

**Sleep
Awareness Week**

Week Beginning
Daylight Savings

The Monday after we lose an hour of sleep for daylight savings time is National Napping Day, and the National Sleep Foundation's Sleep Awareness Week.

NASA found that pilots who power nap for 26 minutes improve performance and alertness. Try the award-winning **Pzizz** app or just set your phone timer for a few minutes of daytime shuteye to recharge.

Work Through Challenges with an AI Therapist

May is National Mental Health Awareness Month. Download the **Woebot** app to let artificial intelligence help with your anxiety, negative thinking, "stuck-ness," relationship management and more. It's not quite as weird as it sounds, and it's free. **Intellect** is an award-winning app that uses the same AI principles. And **Wysa** has positive reviews as well.

Intellect
AI Mental Health
Guidance Counselor
intellect.co

Woebot
Artificial Intelligence Mental
Health Chatbot
woebothealth.com

Wysa
AI-Powered Therapy Bot
wysa.io

MAY

**National
Mental Health
Awareness Month**

STAY HEALTHY

Let Go of Negative Thoughts

● ●

Pixel Thoughts

60-Second Mindfulness Break that Visualizes Your Stresses Floating Away

pixelthoughts.co

Scream into the Void

Stress Break and Anger Management Tool in One

screamintothevoid.com

JULY

Toss Away the "Could Haves" and "Should Haves" Day

Third Saturday in July

The third Saturday in July is Toss Away the "Could Haves" and "Should Haves" Day, a reminder to let go of the little voices inside of us who say we should be doing more.

Two fun sites will help put your challenges into perspective: **Pixel Thoughts** and **Scream into the Void**. Both sites let you secretly share a frustration, but they have very different ways of helping you let the negative thought go. I won't spoil the fun by revealing their methods. Give them a try when you're overwhelmed.

Pets

Take a Walk with Your Pups

Let me see if I have this straight: February 22 is National Walking the Dog Day, but Walk Your Dog Month is January. And then National Walk Your Dog Week is the first week of October.

Well, that should cover the simple act of finding the leash, calming the dog down enough to clip to the collar and starting down your driveway for a brisk walk with your pup.

Whichever date you celebrate, do it with **WoofTrax**. Dogs need walks. Animal shelters need donations. Doesn't it make sense to link these two needs? WoofTrax lets you turn your afternoon puppy outings into fundraising opportunities for your favorite shelters.

WoofTrax Walk for a Dog

Activity Tracker that Benefits Animal Shelters

wooftrax.com

 JANUARY

Walk Your Dog Month

 FEBRUARY 22

National Walking the Dog Day

 OCTOBER 1–7

National Walk Your Dog Week

Help Your Pet in an Emergency

Red Cross Pet First Aid

App for Emergency Treatment for Animals

Text "GETPET" to 90999

 APRIL

National Pet First Aid Awareness Month

April is National Pet First Aid Awareness Month. There's an app for that: **Red Cross Pet First Aid**.

This app helps you identify and evaluate pet emergencies with questions to determine what's wrong and step-by-step advice on first aid. It's like having a veterinary hotline at your fingertips.

Find Dog-Friendly Businesses

BringFido

Directory of Pet-Friendly Businesses

bringfido.com

 JUNE

Take Your Dog to Work Day

Friday after Father's Day

Woof! June 24 is Take Your Dog to Work Day, and anyone who celebrates this holiday will also love **BringFido**, a directory of dog-friendly hotels, restaurants and other businesses.

Do Good Things

Charity and Doing Good

Be Kind. Do Kind Things.

Random Acts of Kindness

Site with Inspiration for Daily Kindnesses

randomactsofkindness.org

FEBRUARY 17

Random Acts of Kindness Day

FEBRUARY

Random Acts of Kindness Week

Week of February 17

We have an official Random Acts of Kindness Week and a Random Acts of Kindness Day. And if that is not enough, the **Random Acts of Kindness** website has ideas for kindness for every day of the year.

The website will make you feel warm all over. Not only does it have do-good inspiration in the blog posts, but you'll also find dozens of downloads to spread kindness, including daily calendars, coloring pages for kids and inspirational posters and posts.

Help Stop Human Trafficking

January is National Slavery and Human Trafficking Prevention Month. We can all make a difference by taking pictures of hotel rooms in our travels and uploading them to the **TraffickCam** app. The pictures go into a database to help identify locations of trafficked victims.

TraffickCam

App to Help Track Human Trafficking in Hotels

exchangeinitiative.com/ traffickcam

JANUARY

National Slavery and Human Trafficking Prevention Month

Share a Great Book

Dolly Parton's Imagination Library

Initiative to Get Books into Every Kid's Hands Every Month from Birth to Five Years

imaginationlibrary.com

International Book Giving Day

Site that Organizes Book Donations to Kids

bookgivingday.com

 FEBRUARY 14

International Book Giving Day

A nerd sighs with happiness every time someone shares a book, and she leaps for joy when the recipient is a child. National Treasure Dolly Parton founded the **Imagination Library** to make sure kids get books of their own. And the whole purpose of **International Book Giving Day** every February 14th is to collect books around the world to foster literacy.

Pay It Forward

November is National Gratitude Month, a great time of the year to reflect on things we're thankful for and to help others. I could write a whole book with easy ideas to give to charity without much effort at all. Here are a few more:

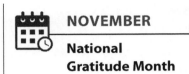

NOVEMBER

National Gratitude Month

Amazon Smile

Amazon Charity Initiative that Lets You Choose a Charity that Will Get a Kickback from Your Purchases

smile.amazon.com

Be My Eyes

Free App that Lets Sighted Volunteers Help Blind and Low-Vision Users with Daily Activities

bemyeyes.com

Charity Miles

Exercise App that Donates to Charity When You Log Miles

charitymiles.org

Tab for a Cause

Chrome Extension that Raises Money for Charity Every Time You Open a New Tab

tab.gladly.io

Write a Real Letter

Love for Our Elders

Site that Connects People with Lonely Elders Who Could Use a Human Connection

loveforourelders.org

 FEBRUARY 26

National Letter to an Elder Day

Sniff. Sniff. Oh, I'm sorry. I was just reading the inspiration behind National Letter to an Elder Day (February 26). It was founded by a kid who loves his grandpa, and he recognized how lonely elders were. So he started a nonprofit called **Love for Our Elders** where you can read the stories of lonely people who just want a few human connections.

Here's where I am supposed to suggest an app so you can write a letter without picking up a pen. You can use the ones on Page 58, but seriously… this site will tug at your heart and inspire you to write an honest-to-goodness note. I just finished up a note for Grandpa White whose wife of 60 years died last year. Sniff.

Waste Time for a Good Cause

Free Rice

Trivia and Educational Quizzes that Earn Money for Charity

freerice.com

 SEPTEMBER 5

International Day of Charity

The International Day of Charity on September 5 is another reminder to keep giving back, and giving back is especially easy when it doesn't cost you a penny.

An oldie but a goodie, **Free Rice** quizzes visitors on vocabulary, science, pop culture and more. When you get an answer right, sponsors donate the equivalent of a few grains of rice to the United Nations' World Food Programme. I love it so much I have to keep it in my no-no list when I use the StayFocusd tool to block time-wasting sites (see Page 21).

Donations and Recycling

Donate Your Old (But Good) Stuff

On March 2, pull the boxes down from the closets and venture into your attic for National Old Stuff Day. After you spend a moment or two on memories, declutter your home by packing up your high-quality goodies to donate.

Give Back Box provides prepaid shipping labels for clothing and household goods you no longer need. Just fill up a box, pack it to the brim (with good quality donations), then drop them in the mail. Charities receive the donations, and sponsors pay for the shipping and handling.

Give Back Box
Program for Donations via Mail

givebackbox.com

 MARCH 2
National Old Stuff Day

Go Shopping with Your Gift Cards

If you're difficult to buy for, you may have gotten a pile of gift cards for the December holidays. Not only is there a National Use Your Gift Card Day (the third Saturday of January), the founder, Use Your Gift Card, helps you donate your unused cards to the nonprofit **Gift Card Bank**.

Gift Card Bank
Site for Donating the Gift Cards You've Been Collecting

giftcardbank.org

 JANUARY
National Use Your Gift Card Day

Third Saturday of January

Recycle and Repurpose Your Old Devices

911 Cell Phone Bank

Phone Recycling and
Repurposing Charity

911cellphonebank.org

AlfredCamera

App to Turn Your Old Devices
into Security Cameras

alfred.camera

Tech for Troops

Veteran Nonprofit that Takes
Device Donations

techfortroops.org

 DECEMBER 17

**National Device
Appreciation Day**

Many people get new smartphones and gadgets during the December gifting season, so I'm not sure why someone thought we should celebrate National Device Appreciation Day on December 17. But it is a good time to take stock of the devices in your desk drawer (or the ones you're thinking of replacing).

You can use your old devices as security cameras with an app like **AlfredCamera** or donate them to charities like **911 Cell Phone Bank** and **Tech for Troops**.

Environment

Turn Off the Lights

The Canadian Energy Efficiency Alliance (CEEA) designated January 10 as National Cut Your Energy Costs Day.

OhmConnect's biggest availability is in California as of now, but it is expanding. Consumers that sign up with the service can earn money back by actively cutting back on energy use during peak periods.

OhmConnect

Cash-Back Program for Cutting Back on Energy Use

ohmconnect.com

 JANUARY 10

National Cut Your Energy Costs Day

Get Out Your Binoculars

eBird

App to Help Record Birds for Great Backyard Bird Count

birdcount.org/ ebird-mobile-app

Great Backyard Bird Count

Grassroots Movement to Track Bird Populations

birdcount.org

iBird

Mobile Field Guide

ibird.com

Merlin Bird ID

Bird Identification App

merlin.allaboutbirds.org

 FEBRUARY

Great Backyard Bird Count

Friday Through Monday Near Valentine's Day (February 14)

Before you start practicing your nerdy pick-up lines for Valentine's Day, grab your binoculars for the **Great Backyard Bird Count**, which is celebrated for four days every February near Valentine's Day.

Volunteers spend the week counting birds to help the Audubon Society monitor bird populations. Take the pledge to volunteer, then download the **Merlin Bird ID** app or use **eBird** to figure out what you're seeing. Not enough bird tools? People also love **iBird** as a field guide for birds.

Clean Out Your Physical Mailbox

Earth Day is April 22, and that's the perfect time to do your part to cut down on junk mail.

I've been using **PaperKarma** for years to snap pictures of unwanted magazines, solicitations and advertisements that fill up my mailbox. PaperKarma submits my name to the companies to be removed from the list. It's well worth the $25 a year. You can also go on an unsubscribe spree for $3.99 for a month.

PaperKarma

App to Unsubscribe from Paper Catalogs and Junk Mail

paperkarma.com

 APRIL 22

Earth Day

Take Small Steps to Help the Planet

Since 1974, the organizations behind World Environment Day (June 5) have been encouraging people everywhere to address critical environmental issues.

Take the first step to doing your part with **Earth Hero**, an app that helps you calculate your carbon footprint and offers suggestions and ideas for living a greener life.

Earth Hero

Environmental App to Make Important Changes

earthhero.org

 JUNE 5

World Environment Day

Save on Paper and Ink

Print Friendly

Site and Chrome Extension that Removes Clutter from Web Pages for Cleaner PDFs and Hard Copies

printfriendly.com

 NOVEMBER 11

National Origami Day

If you print out articles or info from websites, chances are you'll have a stack of paper ready to celebrate National Origami Day on November 11 because of all the extra ads, graphics and miscellaneous stuff. **Print Friendly** eliminates the paper waste by removing clutter from web pages so you print just the info you need without killing all the trees and eating all your printer ink.

Enjoy Life

Food and Beverages

Figure Out What's for Dinner

Allrecipes Dinner Spinner
Recipe Inspiration App
allrecipes.com

Dish Dish
Family Recipe Collection Tool
dishdish.us

Paprika
Recipe Management System
paprikaapp.com

AUGUST 8

National Sneak Some Zucchini onto Your Neighbor's Porch Day

If you've ever grown zucchini squash in your garden, you won't be surprised to hear that on August 8 we celebrate National Sneak Some Zucchini onto Your Neighbor's Porch Day. The plant can explode with zucchini, and you may not have enough squash recipes to use them all.

Allrecipes Dinner Spinner is a favorite app for recipe inspiration. Put in the ingredients you have on hand (such as 17 pounds of zucchini and one stunted carrot), then click the screen to spin. Allrecipes searches the community-built database of recipes for easy, fast meals.

If you're someone who likes to save recipes from the web, check out **Paprika**, a recipe manager that helps you save website recipes with a click, organize your recipes, make meal plans and create grocery lists. And if you're the keeper of Grandpa's Famous Zucchini Jerky recipe, you can create a family cookbook collection with **Dish Dish**.

Pop the Cork on Your Favorite Wine

Believe it or not, Open that Bottle Night has been an official holiday for more than 20 years. On the last Saturday in February, break into that special bottle of wine you're saving for a special occasion. And if you need to find that bottle, try **Vivino**, an app for wine enthusiasts.

Vivino

Wine Picking and Organizing Tool

vivino.com

 FEBRUARY

Open that Bottle Night

Last Saturday in February

Keep Track of Your Favorite Microbrews

When you're taste-testing a flight of microbrews to celebrate National Beer Lover's Day on September 7, use the **Untappd** app to discover new tastes and rate your favorite brews.

Untappd

Beer Rating and Discovery Tool

untappd.com

 SEPTEMBER 7

National Beer Lover's Day

ENJOY LIFE

Celebrate Your Favorite Mixologists

7UP Digital Bartender

Web App to Measure Your
Favorite 7UP Drinks

7up.com/digital-bartender

Cocktail Flow

Site and Apps for
Cocktail Recipes

cocktailflow.com

 **FEBRUARY 24**

World Bartender Day

Modern-day bartenders deserve the elevated title of mixologists because of the creativity and innovation they offer. Visit your favorite watering hole today for one of their liquid masterpieces (and leave a big tip). Then practice your own skills with **Cocktail Flow**, an extensive recipe site for standard and souped-up mixed drinks.

When you're on the go, visit the **7UP© Digital Bartender** site from your phone. Then set your phone on the counter next to your glass. The app shows you the levels to pour your ingredients to in order to make the drink, like this recipe for 7UP Grapefruit Cocktail.

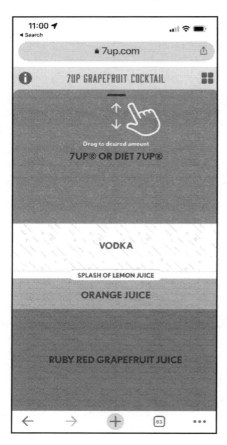

Entertainment

Grab the Remote and the Popcorn

There's so much joy waiting for you every November 30 because it's National Stay at Home Because You're Well Day.

Figure out what your next great binge will be with **JustWatch**, a suggestion tool for streaming entertainment services. Or if you want a dose of nostalgia, flip over to **My 90s TV** for cartoons, commercials, shows, music, news and other video clips from your teen years.

Not your decade? There's also **My 60s TV**, **My 70s TV**, **My 80s TV** and even **My 2000s TV**, individual sites that link together.

JustWatch
Show and Movie Suggestions
Tool for Streaming Services
justwatch.com

My 90s TV
Nostalgic Site with Videos
from the 90s and Links to
Other Decades
my90stv.com

NOVEMBER 30
**National Stay at
Home Because
You're Well Day**

ENJOY LIFE

Remove Ads and Suggested Videos

VideoLink

Clutter-Free YouTube
Viewing Site

video.link

JULY 12

**National
Simplicity Day**

One way to celebrate National Simplicity Day on July 12 is to simplify your YouTube viewing experience. Create a clutter-free viewing experience with a site called **VideoLink**.

Once you paste your YouTube on the site, you'll get a viewing experience without ads, comments or other video suggestions. This is a great hack for teachers and anyone showing a video to a group to avoid potentially embarrassing next video suggestions or inappropriate ads.

Add Controls to Your YouTube Viewer

The first YouTube video was uploaded April 23, 2005. Today you can watch millions of hours of movies, concerts, tv shows and more. Add even more controls to your watching experience with browser extensions **Magic Actions Personalized Movie Theater** and **Enhancer for YouTube**. Magic Actions has a cute user interface that sits in your play bar. You can apply filters and even make the video spin in a circle. But when I installed Enhancer, Magic Actions wouldn't work.

And although Enhancer is much more serious, it had features I liked even better, such as speed controls and a quick volume booster.

Enhancer for YouTube
YouTube Controls
mrfdev.com/enhancer-for-youtube

Magic Actions Personalized Movie Theater
Cuter YouTube Controls
mycinema.pro

 APRIL 23

YouTube Video Anniversary

Music

Make a Mixtape

Gnod
Interactive Site to Discover
Movies, Artists, Books
and More
gnod.com

Kaseta
Site to Make a Virtual Mixtape
kaseta.co

Music-Map
Site to Discover New Artists
Based on Your Interests
music-map.com

 APRIL 11

**National Eight
Track Tape Day**

National Eight Track Tape Day (April 11) may bring you back to the days of shoeboxes filled with the large cassettes and that funny hiss they made in the players. The next generation of music formats, cassette tapes, ushered in the mixtape, a DIY playlist to treasure and gift. Head on over to **Kaseta** to make your virtual mixtape for free.

Mixtapes are all about discovering new music from others. If you need some musical inspiration, check out **Music-Map**, a site where you enter your favorite artist to see an interactive diagram of others you may enjoy. Music-Map is part of **Gnod**, "the global network of discovery." Gnod also helps you discover movies, art, books and more.

Conduct Your Own Orchestra

International Strange Music Day (August 24) is as good a time as any to make music with the **Blob Opera**. Blob Opera is a project through Experiments with Google, an eclectic mix of crazy tech. You interact with the site to control four Blobs as they sing random AI-generated opera sounds. I don't know. It's strange. You gotta see it.

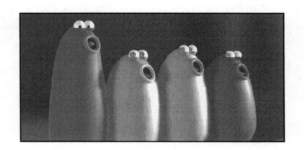

Blob Opera

AI-Powered Interactive Opera Site

experiments.withgoogle.com /blob-opera-on-tour

 AUGUST 24

International Strange Music Day

Make Music with Your Words

OH JOY! October 22 is International Caps Lock Day. Instead of yelling at your coworkers in an email, use your caps lock key on the delightful site called **Typatone**. Just type a phrase, and the site transforms your letters into a melodic tune. A sister site, **Patatap**, adds visuals and animation to your typing.

Patatap

Site that Lets You Type for Musical Graphics

patatap.com

Typatone

Site that Turns Typed Notes into Music

typatone.com

 OCTOBER 22

International Caps Lock Day

Type To Play Jazz

Jazz Keys

AI-Powered Jazz
Music Generator

nerdybff.com/jazzkeys

 APRIL 30

**International
Jazz Day**

Turn a short note into an original jazz tune with **Jazz Keys**. As you type, AI simulates piano music in a jazzy, snazzy way. It's the perfect way to celebrate International Jazz Day on April 30.

Type To Drum

TypeDrummer

Site that Turns Typing
into Drumming

typedrummer.com/j14h26

 MAY

**International
Drum Month**

The powerhouse of percussion instruments gets recognition the whole month of May because it's International Drum Month!

Like Jazz Keys, **TypeDrummer** asks you to type something to create some beats.

Mix Some Old School Beats

MCA Day celebrates the life of late Beastie Boys icon Adam Yauch, aka MCA, who lost his battle to cancer on May 4, 2012. If you were a fan, perhaps you still want to "fight… for your right… to paarrty…."

Try your hand at the Beastie Boys' sound with **808303studio**, an online replica of the old Roland's 808 beats machine that the Boys loved so much.

808303studio

Online Beats Machine

808303.studio

MAY 4(ISH)

MCA Day

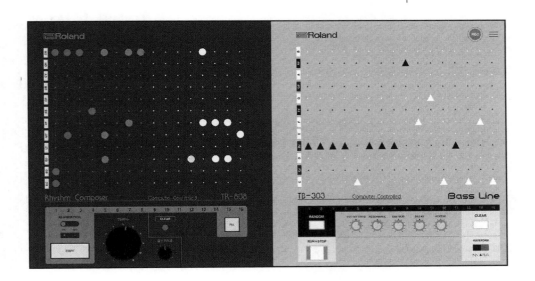

Compose Masterpieces with the Masters

Assisted Melody

Classical Music Generator
Based on the Musical Masters

**nerdybff.com/
assistedmelody**

APRIL 18

**interNational
Organ Day**

Now for a little classical with a side order of education. Play a few notes with your keyboard, and **Assisted Melody** will apply a harmony in the style of a legendary composer. Perhaps start with Bach, who considered the organ "the king of instruments." That's why interNational [sic] Organ Day (April 18) is the perfect day to play.

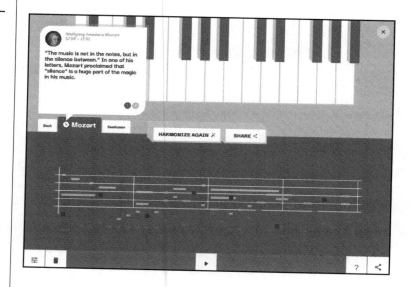

Fun and Games

Play a Vintage Video Game Online

If you look at the famous video game character's name carefully, you can see why MarIO inspired National Mario Day on March 10. Spend an hour or two going back in time with **MyEmulator.online's** retro game collection.

MyEmulator.online

Free Emulator Site for Retro Video Games

myemulator.online

 MARCH 10

National Mario Day

Play a Game of Solitaire

In 1990, Microsoft rolled out Windows 3.0 and included **Microsoft Solitaire** to help new computer users learn how to use the mouse. For its 25th anniversary, Microsoft declared May 22 to be National Solitaire Day. More than 30 years later, the game still has 35 million players a month and is a member of the World Video Game Hall of Fame.

Getting nostalgic? You can also play online.

Microsoft Solitaire Collection

Original Microsoft Solitaire Games

zone.msn.com/en/ mssolitairecollection

 MAY 22

National Solitaire Day

Source:
World Video Game
Hall of Fame at
The Strong

Find Your Inner Child with Legos

Brickit

App that Calculates Lego Bricks and Suggests Projects

brickit.app

JANUARY 28

International Lego Day

January 28 is International Lego Day!

Break out the **Brickit** app to scan your Lego collection so the Brickit app can suggest things you can create from the bricks you have.

Exchange Paper Planes with People Around the World

Fold 'N Fly

Paper Airplane Instruction Site

foldnfly.com

Origami Way

Origami Art Instruction Site

origamiway.com

Paper Planes World

Mobile Site to Create World-Traveling Digital Paper Planes

paperplanes.world

MAY 26

National Paper Airplane Day

No doubt you've folded a paper airplane at some point in your life. Celebrate National Paper Airplane Day on May 26 with a delightful site called **Paper Planes World**. Visit on your phone to add a location stamp to a piece of paper. Then you use your fingers to "fold" the airplane and launch it. You'll see a net pop up so you can catch one to see the other stamps. Then you add yours and relaunch.

When you get all nostalgic and want to build a real plane, head to **Fold 'N Fly**, a site with paper airplane instructions with filters for skill level and behaviors like aerobatics or speed.

And if you get even more nostalgic, check out the hundreds of folded paper activities on **Origami Way**.

Quick Reference Guide

Capture Handwritten Notes from a Real Notebook   17

Rocketbook
Smart Notebook to Save Handwritten Notes to the Cloud
getrocketbook.com

Save Favorite Articles to Read at Your Convenience   17

Pocket
Tool to Save Stuff to Read Later
getpocket.com

Map Out a New Plan   18

Creately
Online Mind Map Tool with Easy Templates
creately.com

MeisterTask
Task Management Tool with Mind Map Integration
meistertask.com

MindMeister
Mind Map Tool with Task Integration
mindmeister.com

Mindmup
Super Simple, Super Free Mind Map Site
mindmup.com

STAY FOCUSED   19

Distraction Management   20

Take Back Your Time   20

Marinara Timer
Online Pomodoro Timer for Groups
marinaratimer.com

Pomodoro Technique®
Kitchen Timer Productivity Technique
cirillocompany.de/pages/ pomodoro-technique

Dive into Deep Work   21

Caveday
Guided Focus Sessions via Zoom
caveday.org

Block Out Your Distractions   21

BlockSite
Free (and Funny) Distraction Helper for Devices and Browsers
blocksite.co

Stayfocusd
Simple Website Blocker with an Attitude
stayfocusd.com

QUICK REFERENCE

Outsourcing 27

Find an Extra Set of Hands 27

Fancy Hands

U.S.-Based Virtual Assistants for Small Tasks

fancyhands.com

Fiverr

Freelance Marketplace for Small Jobs
Starting at Five Bucks

fiverr.com

Upwork

Freelance Community for Larger Projects

upwork.com

Find Skilled Help for Home and Work 28

Thumbtack

Freelancer Marketplace for Projects
and Experts

thumbtack.com

Get a Real Human on the Phone for Customer Service 28

GetHuman

Reference Site for Customer Service Numbers,
Shortcuts, Answers and More

gethuman.com

STAY SAFE 29

Passwords and Security 30

Check to See If Your Email Has Been Breached 30

Have I Been Pwned?

Search Engine for Hacked Emails
and Usernames

haveibeenpwned.com

Upgrade Your Passwords 31

1Password

Top Password Manager with Offline
Storage and Manual Sync

1password.com

Bitwarden

Password Manager with Generous Free Version

bitwarden.com

Dashlane

Top Password Manager with Online/Offline
Storage Options

dashlane.com

Keeper

Top Password Manager with
Extra Secure Security

keepersecurity.com

LastPass

Beth Z's Favorite Password Manager

lastpass.com

QUICK REFERENCE

File Management   45

Convert Your Files to a New Format   45

Zamzar
File Converter Extraordinaire
zamzar.com

Share Files from One Device to Another   45

Snapdrop
Online Service to Transfer Files Between Devices
snapdrop.net

Back Up Your Computer and Files   46

Acronis Cyber Protect Home Office
Super-Secure Backup System with Ransomware Protection
acronis.com

Microsoft Backup and Restore
Microsoft's Built-In Backup Tool
nerdybff.com/windowsbackup

Paragon Backup & Recovery
Cloud Backup Tool with Free Level for Non-Commercial Use
paragon-software.com

Time Machine
Mac's Built-In Backup Tool
nerdybff.com/timemachine

World Backup Day Pledge
Site with Simple Tips for Backing Up Your Files
worldbackupday.com

Find Your Duplicate Files   48

Duplicate Cleaner for Windows
Windows Duplicate File Finder
digitalvolcano.co.uk/duplicatecleaner.html

Gemini 2
Mac Duplicate File Finder
macpaw.com/gemini

Stop the Frantic Searches for the Files You Need for Today's Meeting   48

Searchable.ai
Multi-App Search Engine to Find Files, Emails, Chats and More No Matter Where They Live
searchable.ai

Utilities   49

Discover If a Website Is Down   49

Down Detector
Real-Time Problem and Outage Monitoring
downdetector.com

Down for Everyone or Just Me?
Site that Checks to See If Websites Are Down
downforeveryoneorjustme.com

Autofill Your Cookie Consent   50

Super Agent
Browser Extension to Opt Out of Website Cookies Automatically
super-agent.com

QUICK REFERENCE

QUICK REFERENCE

MEET BETTER   69

Online Meeting Tools   70

Host Asynchronous Meetings   70

Comeet
Asynchronous Meeting Tool
comeet.me

Put a Little Zip in Your Zoom   71

Zoom
The Videoconference Tool that Became a Verb
zoom.com

Try an Online Video Tool that Isn't Zoom   72

Around
Conversational (and Cute) Online Meeting and Hanging Out Tool
around.co

See Your Connections Face to Face   72

mmhmm
Zoom Alternative with Creative Graphic Interface and Fun Personality
mmhmm.app

OOO
Video Meeting Tool with Creative Backgrounds and Fun Interface
ooo.mmhmm.app

Use an AI Helper to Take Notes for You   73

Perfect Recall
Zoom Meeting Recorder with Live Transcript, Note-Taking and Video Highlights
perfectrecall.app

Meeting Engagement   74

Start Your Next Zoom Meeting with an Icebreaker   74

Zoom Apps
Marketplace of Fun and Functional Apps that Integrate with Zoom
nerdybff.com/zoomapps

Host a Scavenger Hunt   74

GooseChase
Scavenger Hunt Tool for Team Bonding in Person or Online
goosechase.com

Add More Fun to Your Online Meetings   75

Flippity
Engagement Tools for Meetings and More
flippity.net

Share Images with Guests at an Event   75

LiveShare
Photo-Sharing Tool for Events
livesharenow.com

QUICK REFERENCE

QUICK REFERENCE

Design Templates 94

Add a Twist to Your Social Media Graphic Templates 94-95

Canva
The World's Best Graphic Template Tool
canva.com

Picmaker
Graphic Template Tool with
AI-Powered Design Ideas
picmaker.com

Instantly Update Your Graphics 96

Biteable Image Resizer
Site that Instantly Transforms Images into the
Right Size for Any Social Media Platform
biteable.com/tools/image-resizer

Designify
Site that Applies 70+ Layouts to
an Image in Seconds
designify.com

Download All Images
Chrome Extension to Download Images
from a Site in One Click
download-all-images.mobilefirst.me

PhotoRoom
App that Applies 70+ Layouts to
an Image in Seconds
photoroom.com

Design Tools 97

Let AI Help Your Sketching Skills 97

AutoDraw
Google's AI-Powered Doodle Recognition Tool
autodraw.com

Quick, Draw!
Google Pictionary-Type Challenge
quickdraw.withgoogle.com

Generate Fake Faces 98

Generated Photos
Site to Generate AI Faces of People
Who Don't Exist
generated.photos

GIF Yourself 99

Removeit.io
Watermark-Free Video Background Remover
removeit.io

Unscreen
Original Site to Remove Video Backgrounds
unscreen.com

Try Out Some New Color Schemes 99

Adobe Color
Adobe's Color Palette Generator
color.adobe.com

Coolors
Fun and Flexible Color Palette Generator
coolors.co

QUICK REFERENCE

Illustrate Your Points with Sketchnotes or Whiteboard Videos   106

Concepts
Sketchnote and Illustration Note App

concepts.app

Doodly
Whiteboard, Blackboard and Glassboard Software

doodly.com

Powtoon
Online Whiteboard and Explainer Video Tool

powtoon.com

VideoScribe
Downloadable Whiteboard Video Tool

videoscribe.co

Add Captions to Your Videos   107

Milk Video
Online Auto-Captioning Video Tool for Video Clips from Meetings

milkvideo.com

Wave.video
Social Media Video Tool with AI-Powered Animated Captions

wave.video

Animate Your Messages   108

Animaker
Animation Site with Robust Free Options

animaker.com

Steve.ai
Animation Site for Text-to-Video AI Creations

steve.ai

Royalty-Free Images, Audio and Video   109

Discover Interesting, Unusual and Gigantic Royalty-Free Collections   109

Bigger Collections   *110*

Library of Congress
Collection of Images, Books, Audio, Videos and More that the Library of Congress Believes Are Free to Use

loc.gov/free-to-use

New York Public Library Public Domain Collections
Public Domain Downloads with the Coolest Visualization Tools Ever

nypl.org/research/collections/digital-collections/public-domain

Unsplash
Legendary Free Image Site

unsplash.com

Wikimedia Commons
50M+ Free Media Files in a Clunky Search Interface

commons.m.wikimedia.org

Icons   *110*

3Dicons
Free 3D Icons in Multiple Formats and Angles

3dicons.co/

Icons8
Insane Number of Customizable Illustrations, Images, Music, 3D Files. Insane.

icons8.com

Photos   *111*

Canadian Stock Images

Funny (and Free) Stock Images
with a Decidedly Canadian Vibe

cira.ca/stock-images

Foodiesfeed

Free Royalty-Free Stock Images of Food

foodiesfeed.com

From Old Books

Free Images from Antique and Vintage Books

fromoldbooks.org

Kaboompics

Beautiful Images with Amazing
Search Engine and Color Palette Analyses

kaboompics.com

SplitShire

High-Quality Free Photos and Video

splitshire.com

Illustrations   *112*

3D Bay

Free, Fun 3D Stock Images

clouddevs.com/3dbay/

Blush

Free and Premium Customizable Character
Illustrations with Scenes

blush.design

Iconduck

More than 100k Free Royalty-Free Icons
with a Super Search Engine

iconduck.com

Audio   *113*

Free Music Archive

Collection of Free Music by Artists

freemusicarchive.org

Freesound

Free Sound Effects and Audio Clips

freesound.org

Uppbeat

Free and Subscription-Based Audio
with Sound Effects and Music

uppbeat.io

YouTube Audio Library

Extensive Collection of Free Royalty-Free
Audio and Sound Effects

youtube.com/audiolibrary

Video   *113*

Cleanpng.com

Free Graphics with Transparent Backgrounds

cleanpng.com

Life of Pix

Royalty-Free Images with a Free Video Cousin

lifeofpix.com

Life of Vids

Royalty-Free Videos with a Free Image Cousin

lifeofvids.com

NegativeSpace

Well-Composed, Hi-Res Photos

negativespace.co

Videvo

Mix of Free and Paid Video Clips
and Stock Footage

videvo.net

Put on a Smiley Face   114

Emojipedia
Directory of Emojis with Trends and Variations
emojipedia.org

Freepik
Millions of Vectors, Images, Icons, Themes and Much More
freepikcompany.com

Reshot
100% Free Royalty-Free Icons, Illustrations and Images
reshot.com

SPEND AND SAVE   115

Travel   116

What's Next? Beach or Mountains?   116

Hopper
Travel Shopping App to Find the Best Time to Fly
hopper.com

Skyscanner
Travel Tool for People with Wanderlust
skyscanner.com

Change Your View Without Leaving Home   117

WindowSwap
Site for Views from Windows Around the World
window-swap.com

Meet Your Family for Dinner   117

WhatsHalfway.com
Site to Find Restaurants, Hotels and Other Meetup Places Between Two Points
whatshalfway.com

Plan a Road Trip   118

iExit
Interstate Exit Guide
iexitapp.com

Roadtrippers
Road Trip Planner
roadtrippers.com

Track Your Mileage Automatically   119

Hurdlr
Mileage Tracker for the Gig Economy
Hurdlr.com

MileIQ
Original Automatic Mileage Tracker App
mileiq.com

Stride
Free Mileage Tracker Tool with Expense Management
stridehealth.com/tax

Emergency and First Aid   162

Brush Up on Your First Aid Skills   162

Red Cross First Aid App
App for Training and Advice for First Aid
Text "GETFIRST" to 90999

Red Cross First Aid Smart Speaker Tool
Smart Speaker First Aid Advice and Training
Enable on Alexa or Google Assistant

Prepare for Emergencies   163

FEMA App
FEMA's Mobile Resources for Emergency
Preparedness and Help
fema.gov

Ready
U.S. Government Site for Disaster
Preparedness and Resources
ready.gov

what3words
Precise Location System for Every 3-Meter
Square in the World
what3words.com

Self-Care and Mental Health   164

Retreat and Recover   164

SoundPrint
Sound-Level Measuring App that Helps You
Find Quiet Places to Work
soundprint.co

Take a Deep Breath   164

Breathe from Calm
Site for Deep Breathing Exercises
calm.com/breathe

eXHALeR
Customizable Breathing Exercises Online
xhalr.com

Get a Good Night's Sleep   165

10 Percent Happier
Positive Podcast for Help with Self Care
tenpercent.com

Calm
Mediation and Sleep Tools
calm.com

Headspace
Another Meditation and Sleep Tool
headspace.com

Insight Timer
Meditation and Sleep Platform
with Free Options
insighttimer.com

Sleep Meditations for Women
Free Meditations and Sleep Help Focused
on a Female Audience
womensmeditationnetwork.com

Take a Power Nap   166

Pzizz
Sleep Management App
pzizz.com

Work Through Challenges with an AI Therapist   167

Intellect
AI Mental Health Guidance Counselor
intellect.co

Woebot
Artificial Intelligence Mental Health Chatbot
woebothealth.com

Wysa
AI-Powered Therapy Bot
wysa.io

Let Go of Negative Thoughts   168

Pixel Thoughts
60-Second Mindfulness Break that Visualizes Your Stresses Floating Away
pixelthoughts.co

Scream Into the Void
Stress Break and Anger Management Tool in One
screamintothevoid.com

Pets   169

Take a Walk with Your Pups   169

WoofTrax Walk for a Dog
Activity Tracker that Benefits Animal Shelters
wooftrax.com

Help Your Pet in an Emergency   170

Red Cross Pet First Aid
App for Emergency Treatment for Animals
Text "GETPET" to 90999

Find Dog-Friendly Businesses   170

BringFido
Directory of Pet-Friendly Businesses
bringfido.com

DO GOOD THINGS   171

Charity and Doing Good   172

Be Kind. Do Kind Things.   172

Random Acts of Kindness
Site with Inspiration for Daily Kindnesses
randomactsofkindness.org

Help Stop Human Trafficking   173

TraffickCam
App to Help Track Human Trafficking in Hotels
exchangeinitiative.com/traffickcam

Share a Great Book   174

Dolly Parton's Imagination Library
Initiative to Get Books into Every Kid's Hands Every Month from Birth to Five Years
imaginationlibrary.com

International Book Giving Day
Site that Organizes Book Donations to Kids
bookgivingday.com

App Index

Holidays and the NerdHerd

You've made it to the end of the book! Congratulations. My husband never reads my books because, as he says, they don't have a plot.

The True Meaning of Nerd365

The title of this book is "Nerd365: A Year of APP-ortunities to Upgrade Your Life," and I want to help you plan out your year no matter when you start this book. This section includes a month-by-month guide to occasions that match up with the tech tips and tools.

But wait! There's more.

This QR code brings you to the calendar page on our site where you can check out the calendar and all the tips. You can even subscribe to Nerd365 to put the tips on your personal calendar.

Celebrate the NerdHerd

This section also contains the names of all the people who pre-ordered this book, affectionately known as my NerdHerd. They are listed in their birthday months, but I celebrate them all year long.

January

January

Here and There

First Day of Month	National Journal Writing Month	*87*
Second Full Week	Universal Letter Writing Week	*58*
Second Monday	National Clean Off Your Desk Day	*14*
Second Tuesday	National Shop for Travel Day	*116*
Second Saturday	National Vision Board Day	*86*
Third Thursday	Get to Know Your Customers Day	*59*
Third Saturday	National Use Your Gift Card Day	*177*
Last Tuesday	National Plan for Vacation Day	*116*
Fourth Wednesday	Library Shelfie Day	*142*
Last Monday	National Bubble Wrap Appreciation Day	*14*
Last Friday	National Fun at Work Day	*74*
Last Business Week	Clean Out Your Inbox Week	*41*

NerdHerd January Birthdays

Ann Hutchison

Barbara Cobuzzi

Batman's Wife

Cheryl Sullivan

Chris Daily

Cory Davis

Darren Curry

David Littleton

Elizabeth Green

Erica Meyer

John Tolson

Judy Oiler

Karen Woodring

Lois Creamer

Mariko Lanicek

Marquesa Pettway, Zoom Queen

Maureen Heisinger

Melissa Kelleher

Micki Novak

Mimi Brown

Nicole Abbott

Rebecca Maalouf

Shannon Carroll

Shawna Korth, Big Sky Brokers

Tami in Louisiana

W. Craig Henry

Wade Koehler

February

Day by Day

All Month

NerdHerd February Birthdays

Anne Lupkoski

Ashley Simon

Cathi Eifert Horner, CAE

Chellie Phillips

Cheryl Meyers

Debbie Li

Donna C. Denley

Jaime Paris

Jeffrey Horn

Judith Briles

Kat Ellermann

Kimberly Semenko

Linda Whale de Vargas

Lisa Farquharson

Penney Howe

RaDonna Hessel

Sara Nash, CAE

Stasia Creek

Steve Reese

Traci Brown

Yasmin Lalani

February

Here and There

March

Day by Day

March

Here and There

Week Beginning Daylight Savings	Sleep Awareness Week	*166*
First Monday after Daylight Savings	National Napping Day	*166*
First Friday	National Day of Unplugging	*22*
First Friday	National Speech and Debate Education Day	*77*
First Week	Telecommuter Appreciation Week	*71*
First Full Week	National Consumer Protection Week	*35*
First Full Week	Words Matter Week	*54*
First Full Week	Read an Ebook Week	*143*

NerdHerd March Birthdays

Alan Wald

Bianca Constance

Catherine Luke

Clarence E. Cox, III

Dale Knutsen

Diann Rogers

Gloria Rossiter

James C. Camacho

Jay Smith

Jennifer Marusak

John Silwonuk

Johnny Pope

Judy Moss

Karen Kirby Smith

Kate Van Auken

Kathy Kuzava

Kimberly Simon Perkins

Kristi Valentine

Lana Homnick-Lee

Lori Ropa

Lori Youker

Louise Smith

Marti Wangen

Michelle Murphey Porter

Teri Carden

April

Day by Day

All Month

April

Here and There

First Day of Month	National Journal Writing Month *87*
Wednesday of the Last Full Week	Administrative Professional Day *27*
Third Thursday	Get to Know Your Customers Day *59*
Date Depends on Hebrew Calendar	Education and Sharing Day *76*

NerdHerd April Birthdays

Alia Snyder

Allan Mendels

Anne Glasscock

Becky McCormack

Brad Anderson

Cheryl Bowie

Christine Hokans

Craig Backus,
Local Search Ninja

Darcy Burnett

Donna Sather

Elizabeth Criswell

Gary Rifkin

Gloria Gibbon

Jami Baker Orr

Jamison Barcelona

Jeanie Hinkle

John Craighill

Justin Sawran

Leslie Fritz

Lowell Aplebaum

Lucy Bottorff

Mara Kolter

Marianne Pettys

Mark Beamis

Megan Mueller

Melissa Blount

Melissa Fetterhoff

Polly Karpowicz

Raquel Vargas-Whale

Rhonda Zunker

Sandra Giarde, CAE

Shana Teehan

Susan Wan-Ross

Tim Houterloot

Wendi Douglas

May

May

Here and There

Friday before Memorial Day National Road Trip Day *118*

First Full Week Update Your Reference Week *81*

First Thursday World Password Day *31*

First Saturday Free Comic Book Day *145*

NerdHerd May Birthdays

Amy Strahan

Ashton Barcelona

Beth Surmont

Calvina King

Carolyn Pennington

Commander Mary Kelly, US Navy (ret)

Deanne DeMarco

Debbie Pate-Newberry

Debby Jones

Donna Rankin

Jean White

Joe Krenowicz

Julie Fuselier

Kimberly Pipes

Lorrie Trogden

Lynn Caccavallo

Mark Dressner

Marsha McGreevey

Nora Y. Onishi

Pam Donahoo

Rebecca L. Turner, REALTOR®

Rita Tayenaka

Trish Neal

Wanda Lowe-Anderson

June

Day by Day

All Month

June

Here and There

First Saturday	National Trails Day	*147*
First Full Week	National Business Etiquette Week	*60*
Second Tuesday	Call Your Doctor Day	*159*
Third Friday	National Take Back the Lunch Break Day	*61*
Last Thursday	National Work from Home Day	*63*
Friday after Father's Day	Take Your Dog to Work Day	*170*

NerdHerd June Birthdays

Carol Morris

Dale Boeckenstedt

Daniel Curtin

Dianne Richards

Emily Garner

Fran Rickenbach, CAE, IOM

Marla Novak

Melissa Heeke

Michele Huber

Mona McCarthy

Pam Auld

Sara Ranney, CAP OM

Sharon NeSmith

Teresa Fuqua

Trudy Bounds

Wayne King

Yvonne A. Hersh, CAE

July

Day by Day

All Month

Here and There

NerdHerd July Birthdays

Chris Champion

Denise M. Smith

Dilip Divecha

Elena Gerstmann

Elizabeth Bartz

Jeanee Gilson

Jeff Morrison

Jennifer Coleman

Jennifer Franco

John Zink

Julie Thomas

Julie Watson

Karen Butler

Kath Fitzpatrick

Kay Riddle Petty

Lynette vonAllmen

Missy Droegemeier

Monica McCorkle

Paige Dumas-LeCesne

Papa Ziesenis

Sharon Dawes

Sonja Wassgren Morgan

Steve Leitch

SueAnn Gilmore

Susan Kurtz

Theresa M. Maddix

August

Day by Day

All Month

NerdHerd August Birthdays

Bailey Bourgeois

Beth Bridges

Beth Q. REALTOR®

Bill King

Candi Rawlins

Cheryl Smith

Cindy Camargo

Clark Jones

Denise Stefanick

Greg Hummel

Jerry Huffman

Joyce Endo

Kimberly Wood

Kitty Collins

Kricket Harrison

Laurie Guest

Lenora Billings-Harris

Marilyn Sessions

Mark L. Brown

Mary Ann McDonald

Melanie Rowls

Mike Chamberlain

Nancy McCulley

Olivia Lobban

Peggy Hoffman

Samantha Greasley

Terry Murphy

YGM Total Resource Campaigns

HOLIDAYS AND THE NERDHERD

September

Day by Day

All Month

September

. . . .

Here and There

Day after Labor Day	National Another Look Unlimited Day	*43*
Monday after Labor Day	National Boss/Employee Exchange Day	*67*
Second Saturday	World First Aid Day	*162*
Third Tuesday	National IT Professionals Day	*30*

NerdHerd September Birthdays

Barbara L. Rambow

Candi Fox

Carol Campbell

Celia Fritz-Watson

Debbie Lowenthal

Jackie Rakers

Janet McEwen

Julie Lynch

Katy Molick

Katy Vickery

Kerri Mertz

Linda Richards, Rae Allen
Media RE Photography

Mark Creffield

Nell Withers McCauley

Pam Wyess

Patti Kungel

Robin O. Brown

Stacey Morris

Susan Bauman

Tim Lord

William Mathews

October

Day by Day

All Month

October

Here and There

First Day of Month	National Journal Writing Month 87
October 1–7	National Walk Your Dog Week 169
Second Monday	National Online Bank Day 125
Second Tuesday	National Face Your Fears Day *77*
Third Thursday	Get to Know Your Customers Day 59
Third Week	National Retirement Security Week 123
Third Week	National Estate Planning Awareness Week 12

NerdHerd October Birthdays

Alan Morasch

Bonnie Davis

Carol Hamilton

Carolyn Phillips

Chris Christensen

Gina Sutherland

Heather Blanchard, CAE

Jeanette Morrish

Jeanette Schlapfer

Joe Ferri

Joyce Pleva

Julie Doughty

Karah Covey

Lisa Van Gemert

Loretta Mingram

Malcolm Sweet

Marcia Clarke, Broker & REALTOR®, Brooklyn Board of REALTORS® (NY)

Mary Iafrate

Melissa Hull

Ronald Sarver

Shellie A. Robles

Sydney Isaac

Trevor Mitchell

Vickie Lester

November

November

Here and There

Day after Thanksgiving   National Day of Listening *73*

First Thursday   International Project Management Day *64*

First Monday   Job Action Day *80*

NerdHerd November Birthdays

Addison Simon

Betty Brock

Bridgette Bienacker

Craig Alexander

Diane Thurber-Wamsley

E. Marie Wilson

freedivedoug

Jenifer Grady

Jill Rasco

Joanne St-Pierre

Julie Kellman

Kandy Cefoldo

Karen McCullough

Kelly Paxton

Kristin Parker

Larry Strazzella

Leslie Remy

Lyle Wolf

Marla Dalton

Marlo Jackson

Robert Newman, CAE, IOM

Ronda Gilliland-Lopez

Stephanie Butler

Vanessa Ignacio

December

Day by Day

All Month

December

Here and There

Last Workday of the Year   No Interruptions Day   *21*

NerdHerd December Birthdays

Barbara Boulton

Betsy Smith

Bette Price

Candy Joyce

Crystal Washington

Cynthia Philbrook

Debra Jason

Dr. Juan Lorenzo

Martinez-Colon

Duane Washkowiak

Heather Pauley

Kevan S. Lyons

Laura De George

Laurie Bourgeois

Monica Waller

Phil Gerbyshak

Portia Metoyer

Sharon Bradley

Skip Koski

Susan Valle

Tim Teehan

Tom Wright

Why you NEED a Nerdy Best Friend...

Do you ever feel like the technology that was supposed to make our lives easier is the very thing making it so complicated?

If you do — you're not alone. Sorting through all the digital clutter to find real, effective solutions to our everyday problems can feel overwhelming.

To find technology to make your life easier, you could hunt for hours, demo for days or Google for greatness.

Or you could just ask Your Nerdy Best Friend.

Beth Ziesenis, Your Nerdy BFF, sorts through the digital clutter to discover tech tips, tools and tricks to solve life's everyday problems. Then she shares her best tips in easy-to-understand short bites with humor and pizzazz online and in person.

Beth takes the fear out of technology and helps you get right to the point with effective apps and tools that you can integrate into your everyday work and life.

Certified Speaking Professional

Beth earned the designation of Certified Speaking Professional, and speaking engagements are the primary way she shares her tips. All Beth Z's sessions include interaction, laughs and learning – both online and in person.

Attendees walk out of the session with tools they can use right away. Your Nerdy Best Friend is not a traditional Zoom box speaker with online programs or "Sage on the Stage" in person. Beth engages attendees with special effects, conversations, funny (nerdy) pictures, social media updates and serious buzz creation.

Find Out If Beth Z Is a Good Fit for Your Event
Site: yournerdybestfriend.com
Email: beth@yournerdybestfriend.com
Phone: 619-231-9225